The Gender Politics of
Educational Change

Educational Change and Development Series

Series Editors: Andy Hargreaves, Ontario Institute for Studies in Education, Canada and Ivor F Goodson, Warner Graduate School, University of Rochester, USA and Centre for Applied Research in Education, University of East Anglia, Norwich, UK

Re-schooling Society
David Hartley

The Gender Politics of Educational Change
Amanda Datnow

The Rules of School Reform
Max Angus

The Gender Politics of Educational Change

Amanda Datnow

 The Falmer Press

(A member of the Taylor & Francis Group)
London • Washington, D.C.

UK   The Falmer Press, 1 Gunpowder Square, London, EC4A 3DE
USA   The Falmer Press, Taylor & Francis Inc., 1900 Frost Road, Suite 101, Bristol, PA 19007

First published in 1998

A catalogue record for this book is available from the British Library

Library of Congress Cataloging-in-Publication Data are available on request

ISBN 0 7507 0705 4 cased
ISBN 0 7507 0629 5 paper

Jacket design by Caroline Archer

Typeset in 10/12pt Garamond
Graphicraft Typesetters Ltd., Hong Kong.

Printed in Great Britain by Biddles Ltd, Guildford and King's Lynn on paper which has a specified pH value on final paper manufacture of not less than 7.5 and is therefore 'acid free'.

Every effort has been made to contact copyright holders for their permission to reprint material in this book. The publishers would be grateful to hear from any copyright holder who is not here acknowledged and will undertake to rectify any errors or omissions in future editions of this book.

Contents

Introduction   1

1 A Framework for Understanding the Gender Politics of
   Educational Change   9

2 Central High School: The Case and its Context   27

3 Teachers at Central High School: Identities and Ideologies   43

4 The Competition over what 'School' Means at Central   78

5 Common and Diverging Themes in the Gender Politics of
   Educational Change   109

6 Implications for School Change   130

Appendix   140

References   148

Index   155

Introduction

In the Fall of 1992, Central High School received over one million dollars from the state to undertake a five-year comprehensive school restructuring effort.[1] Central High School's proposal for restructuring, written by a group of teachers, included a plan to detrack the school by offering all students access to and assistance in a rich and challenging curriculum. Along with detracking, the school had plans to move toward a house structure, homerooms, interdisciplinary thematic instruction, alternative assessment, a customized calendar, a peer-coaching professional development model, and a new governance structure. The restructuring proposal included statements of support from the district office, the school board, and the teachers' union.

Central had money, time, administrative and community support, a coordinated restructuring plan, and a group of teachers who conceived of and wanted the reform, and yet five years later, the status quo prevailed. Central's operating structure was still a traditional one, students were tracked, teachers worked in isolated classrooms and in 1996 the legacy of the proposed novel reforms were nowhere in sight.

School change experts proffer several explanations for failed reform. Some might argue that Central's proposed reforms failed to address the core processes of teaching and learning (Elmore, 1996). Others might believe that the teachers failed to make meaning of the reform (Fullan, 1991) or that Central's restructuring plan did not fully address the context in which the school was located (Sarason, 1990). Finally, it could be that the system and its goals were not stable enough to sustain locally developed reform (Stringfield et al., 1997).

Interestingly, these explanations do not really account for the failure of reform at Central High School. What this book reveals is that reform at Central failed for a very different reason: gender politics. Reform at Central was derailed because a group of veteran male teachers, known as 'the Good Old Boys', strategically and successfully used a crass sexist discourse and their political connections with powerful men in the district to maintain the status quo. The Good Old Boys targeted a group of women teachers who were most active in the reform and were members of the 'Idea Team', the group who developed the restructuring proposal.

We seldom recognize the importance of the seedy underside of school change — the micropolitics. We do not focus on the politics of schools enough, when in fact it is the political dimension of school change that most often causes reform to fail (Hargreaves, Earl and Ryan, 1996; Sarason, 1996). One reason for this is that the language of politics has long been taboo in educational settings (Cuban, 1988; Siskin, 1994). When teachers do use political vocabulary to describe events in their schools, it is used disparagingly to refer to other teachers who emerged victorious in a particular battle. Teachers tend to describe their own actions as motivated by rational interests linked to benefits for children, rather than Machiavellian politics (Siskin, 1994). In reality, reformers in schools are often motivated in part by self-interest, as are defenders of the status quo. However, rarely are either group's motivations couched in blatantly self-referring terms (Mangham, 1979). In sum, the very word 'politics' has negative connotations in schools — and, when used in the same sentence as 'reform', the connotations are worse.

By its very nature, school change is inherently political since education and how it is defined always favor the interests of one constituency over another (Hargreaves, Earl and Ryan, 1996; Sarason, 1996). The truth is, schools are ideologically diverse organizations in which teachers' purposes and beliefs often differ. These differences provide the template for micropolitics in school reform.

This book shows that school reform is not always about the education of children or principles of pedagogy. School change is often about raw politics and internecine warfare among competing interest groups. Reform can become a struggle between factions of teachers over whose definition of 'school' will prevail. The focus of this struggle may not be education, but rather what works in achieving dominance — in the case of Central, it was gender.

This book is the first analysis of gender in the school reform literature. Until now, gender has been treated either as a non-issue or as an organizational pathology in much of the change literature (see Blackmore and Kenway, 1995, p. 237). Historically, studies of school change have overlooked the impact of the relations of power among teachers that revolve around gender (not to mention race and ethnicity) and that undoubtedly affect the change process.

Gender is an important organizing feature of social life in schools. More often than not, it operates as a system of hierarchical relations in which women are commonly accorded less power than men. Gender is a defining feature of teachers' lives. While this was commonly seen to be true at the elementary level, where we often hear of the 'gendered' nature of the teaching profession, it is seldom recognized at the secondary level, much less in school reform. This book brings gender relations among teachers to the forefront in a discussion of school change.

In brief, this book explores a rather novel research question: the relationship of gender to the micropolitics of school change. Several themes are overlaid in a qualitative case study of Central High School: gender, micropolitics, and school reform. In addition to analyzing the school change process at Central, I bring in examples from two other restructuring secondary schools to show that gender factionalism in reform is not unique to Central. As the title indicates, this is a book about the gender politics of educational change.

How are school cultures and structures contested and negotiated in the process of reform? Who has the power to shape schools, and how do these individuals accomplish their goals? Finally, how are professional relationships among teachers influenced by social location, or more specifically, gender? To answer these broad questions, I link micropolitics in school reform to the wider social, economic, and political setting in which the school and individuals are located.

There are several key elements which define the theoretical framework for this study: discourse, ideology, and social location. Discourses shape how we see the world and operate at both the conscious and unconscious levels. Acker (1994) defines discourses as 'systems of representation which circulate a set of meanings' (p. 21). Like other aspects of positionality or social location (e.g., race, social class, age, or ethnicity), gender is embedded in a set of competing discourses, in which the subjectivities of individuals in a setting define how it operates in practice. I use the concept of the politics of representation (Mehan, 1993), which focuses on how discourse can be shifted from one terrain to another by a powerful group in order to achieve domination, as a framework for understanding how gender politics is used as strategy to head off reform. For this reason, I take the language and discourse of the participants in reform very seriously.

Concerning ideology, I believe that teachers come to school with different definitions of what school means and how their roles as teachers ought to be defined. Teachers' contrasting definitions of the school are connected to their sense of self, purpose, career aspirations, and professional identities (Ball, 1987). Not surprisingly then, school reforms, many of which are highly politicized, provoke factionalism among teachers on various grounds. Teachers enter the school reform process with different ideologies, and often those ideologies have their bases in existing teacher subcultures, which can become political factions in reform.

Finally, teachers come to school from different social locations, which vary along gender, racial, socio-economic, historical, and political dimensions (Bahktin, 1981). As teachers struggle to redefine 'school' in the process of reform, their dialogue is mediated by existing power relations, both within school and within society. This is important because not all perspectives are seen as equal; power is not evenly distributed in institutions. The social location, or positionality, of those involved, strongly impacts school reform: 'All people define situations as real; but when powerful people define situations as real, they are real for everybody involved in their consequences' (Mehan, 1990, p. 60).

This book takes seriously the interpretations, interactions, and ideologies of actors in the setting. The story of reform is presented through their voices, as it is through teachers' voices that we begin to understand their lives and purposes (Goodson, 1991). However, these voices are not seen or portrayed as politically neutral. Instead, the voices of educators are placed within the context of the contested power terrain in which they were located. Moreover, while the agency of actors (in this case, teachers) in the process of reform is the primary focus of this book, structural forces both at the school and societal levels are also emphasized, and culture is recognized as a mediating factor (Datnow, 1995). I attempt to acknowledge the large scale institutional forces that arise from social, political, and economic relations. While culture may be characterized as serving a dominant ideology, I recognize that a fragmentation of competing ideologies is produced by social differentiation. In sum, I view the relationship between structure, culture, and agency as a dynamic one, in which social forces and action are dialectically related and mutually constitutive. In the agency of individuals, we see structure and culture; in culture, we see agency and structure; and, in structure, we see agency and culture.

Like the actors in the setting, I, too, am reflexively related to the social situations that I have studied. I do not claim to be politically neutral or value free. Concerning school reform, I am a firm believer that schools are in need of fundamental change so that we can better educate all students. Therefore, my sympathies tend to lie with educators in favor of reform. Concerning gender, I believe that women suffer from systematic social inequities because of their sex, and no doubt this is evident in my writing. However, it is very important to note that I did not conduct data collection with a focus on gender inequalities. Rather, as I describe in Chapter 3, I was involved in a longitudinal qualitative study of Central High School's efforts to detrack, as part of a larger ten-school study of detracking that took place at UCLA. I was surprised at how overt, blatant, and palpable the gender politics were at Central.

Gender politics could not help but become the story of reform there. It was only after completing data collection at Central that I began to read literature on gender and the politics of school reform in order to help me make sense of what had happened at the school. After analyzing the data from two other restructuring schools (Explorer Middle School and Grant High School, described in Chapter 5), I realized that the gender politics at Central High School were not anomalous, and therefore merited being written about.

Although this book focuses on gender politics, it has much broader applicability to all stakeholders in school reform. My hope is that this book opens up the black box of school reform by revealing the everyday struggles of actual participants in the process. There is much to learn about the powerful politics of school change in general and about the diversity of ideologies, identities, and actions of secondary school teachers in reform.

The purpose of this book is *not* to suggest that reformers in schools are always women and resisters to change are always men. Rather, I argue that gender-based factions of teachers form for a reason — they are the result, in part, of the politics of representation, the competition among groups to achieve dominance in representing what 'school' means. Factionalism among teachers, which often happens in reform, can happen on a variety of bases — department affiliation, race, ethnicity, native language, age, etc. — whatever happens to work in a group's effort to achieve dominance. For the Good Old Boys at Central, it was gender. And for the restructuring effort there, it meant demise.

Organization of the Book

Chapters 1 and 2 provide the background and context for the book with a literature review and conceptual framework for understanding the gender politics of educational change, a description of the major site of the study, Central High School, and the methods used in data collection and analysis.

Chapter 1 situates the book within the larger body of research on school change, gender and teaching, and micropolitics. A comprehensive review of the literature in these areas reveals that there is little research on the nexus of gender politics and school reform, particularly in the context of current reform agendas which place an increased burden on teachers to change schools. However, taken together, these areas of literature provide an interesting framework with which to understand the gender politics among teachers in school reform efforts.

Chapter 2 sets the stage for the rest of the book with a description of Central High School and its context, including the demographics of the school, district, and community, and a description of the larger economic, political, and social context in which the school is located. This chapter also includes important background information about how reform started at Central High. The significance of detracking, a major component of the school's restructuring plan, is also discussed in this chapter. A discussion of the case study methods used in data collection and analysis at Central, Explorer, and Grant, as part of a larger study of detracking, *Beyond Sorting and Stratification*, is also included in this chapter.

Chapters 3 and 4 describe the gender politics at Central High School. Chapter 3 introduces the reader to the three groups of teachers at Central High School: the 'Idea Team', a faction made up mostly of female teachers, who fought against the current structure and culture in their struggle to bring about detracking; the 'Good Old Boys', a faction of entrenched male teachers, who defended the status quo in the school, including tracking and the dominant ideology that holds it in place; and, the 'Middle Group', a group of teachers who resisted political involvement in the reform. The profile, identity, and ideology of each group of teachers are discussed. In the profile section, each group and its members are described in detail in terms of their individual characteristics and how they define themselves as a group. Because ideology is a theme of micropolitical analysis and is revealing about the role of teachers in reform, this chapter also includes information about teachers' ideologies in each of the factions.

Chapter 4 deals with the intersection of gender, micropolitics, and school reform as it pertains to Central High School. This chapter discusses the interaction of the three groups of teachers in the struggle to define what 'school' means at Central. This chapter is organized both to illuminate the gender political strategy used by teachers in the politics of representation as well as to show the sequence of political action at Central. In doing so, key issues in the literature on the micropolitics of school change and gender that were raised in Chapter 2 are brought to bear in light of the interaction among the factions.

Chapter 5 uses data from two other detracking schools, Explorer Middle School and Grant High School, to describe the gender politics of educational change in other contexts. In this chapter, I describe the reform efforts and gender politics at each school, highlighting the common and diverging themes that exist across these two schools and Central. The situation at these schools most notably differed from Central in that gender politics impacted the course of reform and the school climate in some unproductive ways, but did not derail reform efforts all together.

In Chapter 6, the concluding chapter of the book, I summarize the theoretical and practical implications of this book, primarily discussing what the findings of this book mean for secondary school reform and for future studies of school change.

Acknowledgments

The educators portrayed in this book taught me a tremendous amount about school reform, and I am greatly indebted to them for openly sharing with me their trials and tribulations in reform over the period of several years. It is my hope that educators and researchers around the world will learn as much as I did from the struggles of both the teachers who fought for reform and those who defended the status quo. If this book serves to enlighten us all to the politics of school reform, and the powerful role of gender in shaping those politics, then its purpose will be achieved.

Sincere thanks is due to Andy Hargreaves and the kind group at Falmer Press, including Malcolm Clarkson, Anna Clarkson, and Ivor Goodson for making the publication of this book a reality. Andy Hargreaves, especially, has been the most powerful force in convincing me that a book about the gender politics of educational change would be worth writing and worth reading.

This book evolved from my dissertation, which I completed at the UCLA School of Education under the excellent, unending support and tutelage of Jeannie Oakes and Amy Stuart Wells. In addition to supervising my dissertation, they provided me with the opportunity to spend three very interesting years working with them on a study of ten detracking schools, in which Central High School, Explorer Middle School, and Grant High School were participants. They also allowed me the freedom to use the data from this study for the purposes of this book. Special thanks also to Diane Hirshberg and Karen Ray for sharing their insights about Explorer and Grant with me, and to Irene Serna and Susan Yonezawa for kindly sending me disks and files from the study archives and for assisting in data collection at Central.

Thanks are also due to my colleagues at the Center for Social Organization of Schools at Johns Hopkins University who have helped make this project possible. Particular thanks to Sam Stringfield for constantly reminding me that I had to finish this book; Nettie Legters for engaging me in interesting dialogue about teachers in reform; Florrie

Snively for helping me code data and for faithfully proofreading chapters; and, Karen Dodds for preparing my bibliography and proofreading chapters.

Bud Mehan, who deserves special mention as my first (and a continuing) mentor in the field of education, served as a source of inspiration for a key concept which shapes this book, the politics of representation. Numerous other friends and colleagues have also provided me with much encouragement along the way: Jenny and Jim Antony, Diane Friedlaender, Lea Hubbard, Erin Horvat, Russell and Robinson Katz, Sheila Keegan, Barbara McHugh, and Tina Nishida.

Last but not least, my family deserves much thanks. My parents, my grandmother, and my brother were wonderfully warm and encouraging throughout the project, often kindly reminding me to sleep, eat, and enjoy life. My in-laws were also very supportive of this project, providing me with some insight into the publishing process. Finally, and most importantly, this book is dedicated to husband and partner in life, Jon, who, unlike the aforementioned list of people, actually had to live with me during my successes and frustrations with this book (and its previous incarnation, my dissertation). Jon provided me with not only lots of love, home-cooked meals, and delightful companionship as I wrote, but also provided sage and careful technical and content editing advice.

Data collection for this volume, conducted as part of the 'Beyond Sorting and Stratification' study, was supported by the Lilly Endowment. Preparation of this volume was supported by a grant from the Office of Educational Research and Improvement, U.S. Department of Education, to the Center for Research on the Education of Students Placed At Risk at Johns Hopkins and Howard Universities (Grant No. R117D-40005). However, any opinions expressed in this book are my own, and do not represent the policies or positions of the funders.

Note

1   The name Central High School is a pseudonym for the actual name of the school. Pseudonyms are used for all school, place, and respondent names, in order to protect their anonymity.

1   A Framework for Understanding the Gender Politics of Educational Change

This chapter situates this book about the gender politics of educational change within extant research on the following three areas: school change, gender and teaching, and the micropolitics of schools. I start with a review of the research on school change and how it contributes to our knowledge of the meaning of reform for teachers. I then review the significance of the culture of the school and existing power relationships among individuals in shaping the school change process. I argue that the literature on the school change process oversimplifies the role of teacher agency in reform and portrays culture as monolithic and shared, downplaying the importance of the micropolitical struggles that may ensue as teachers with varying ideologies grapple with reform. Most importantly, I critique the inattention to gender in the school change literature, arguing that what we have learned about the role of gender in teachers' work lives is significant in shaping the process of school change.

To round out my review, I use a micropolitical perspective which focuses on the conflict between interest groups, ideological diversity, and political action to address the power and politics of school reform. I propose that we understand gender politics by looking at the politics of representation, the competition among factions over the meaning of objects or events. The key to the politics of representation is the connection between power and discourse. Taken together with the literature on school change and gender, this provides the necessary framework to explain the role of gender politics in affecting reform.

I now turn to a discussion of the school change literature, focusing on the powerful assumptions about teacher agency in creating successful school reform.

Assumptions about Teacher Agency in School Reform

Teachers are considered by most policymakers and school change experts as the centerpiece of educational change. Therefore, not surprisingly, most reform efforts are directed at teachers, and the involvement of teachers in the school reform process is seen as critical by school change theorists. Policies aimed at decentralization, including grant maintained schools in the UK, charter schools in the US, and self-managing schools in New Zealand, to name a few, all rely on teachers to 'reinvent' school. This belief that teachers have *agency*, the capacity to change the existing state of affairs, has informed reform agendas beginning in the mid-eighties. These reform agendas have emphasized upgrading standards for teachers, providing incentives linked to student achievement, and restructuring schools in order to give teachers a greater role in decision making. This formula for reform has continued into the 1990s, with the emergence of the systemic reform movement (Smith and O'Day, 1991). In sum, policy makers suggest that teachers have the capacity to dramatically improve schools; all they need is freedom at the local level to do so.

School change experts also echo the belief that schools are best changed from the bottom up (Fullan, 1991; Heckman and Peterman, 1997; Sikes, 1992; Wideen, 1994). After all, change efforts which involve imposed, top-down mandates of externally developed curricular innovations have proven to create great dissatisfaction among teachers and ultimately lead to no change at all (Sikes, 1992). Therefore, teachers need to 'own' the process of change, and reform efforts need to be grounded in an understanding of teachers' lives and development (Fullan and Hargreaves, 1996; Hopkins and Wideen, 1984; McNeil, 1988; Sikes, 1992). If teachers are involved in planning and implementing reform, they will find it meaningful, rather than attributing it to the actions of others. Furthermore, when teachers are involved in the change process, it is more likely that important and useful ways of formulating and solving problems will surface (Sarason, 1996).

According to school change experts, teachers must not wait for the system to change, they must push for the kind of professional culture they want through 'skilled change agentry' (Fullan, 1993). The change literature emphasizes the need for 'indigenous invention' in which those inside the school bring about meaningful school reform (Heckman and Peterman, 1997; Sirotnik and Oakes, 1986). In the process of indigenous invention, teachers critically examine their current educational practices and create local solutions for school improvement and a means for assessing their progress. Through this locally developed process of school improvement, teachers arrive at the 'empowered school' (Hargreaves and Hopkins, 1991). In sum, teachers are seen as very active agents, capable of making a significant difference to the existing state of affairs at their schools. Thus, the job of restructuring schools rests, to a large extent, upon their shoulders. In this way, recent reform agendas tap into fundamental societal beliefs about individualism and grass-roots notions of change (Alexander, 1987).

Although a teacher-centered approach is fundamental to successful school change, it has some limitations. Most notably, the assumption that 'teachers can change the world' has one major shortcoming: it does not recognize the dynamic nature of the school reform process and the complex realities of locally developed school reform. Certainly, as the literature points out, teachers are not just pawns in the reform process but are active agents in reform. Success is not simply guaranteed when teachers 'buy into' new ideas. In fact, teachers act in a variety of ways in response to reforms: some teachers push or sustain reform efforts; others resist or actively subvert these efforts. Yet we know very little about how teachers take on these different roles in reform, particularly resistance, or about how teachers with antagonist roles and ideologies grapple with the day-to-day process of school change. In sum, the notion that teachers can change the world does not take into account the negotiations that happen among teachers at the local level as they struggle to redefine what 'school' means for students.

School Culture and the Process of Change

Undoubtedly the culture of the school plays an extremely important role in influencing the politics of reform among teachers. Although the politics of educational change is often not explicitly addressed, the school change literature provides insight into how the culture of the school impacts reform efforts (e.g., Lipman, 1997; Sarason, 1996; Stoll and Fink, 1996). The school change literature correctly highlights that schools have distinct cultures which must be understood because these cultures impact the role of teachers in reform efforts. The success of school reform often relies upon 'reculturing' in addition to restructuring, as the school culture may serve to hold in place organizational structures which inhibit school improvement (Hargreaves, 1994). Finally, changing school cultures requires a deconstruction of hierarchical power relationships. Each of these key points is discussed in more detail below.

School change theorists argue that every school has its own culture which is socially constructed by the members within it (Fullan, 1991; Lieberman, 1995; Sarason, 1990; Stoll and Fink, 1996). For these theorists, the school culture includes shared meanings among educators about the role of school in society, the organizational structure within the school, and the climate for change. This shared school culture, in simple terms, is 'the way we do things around here' (Deal and Kennedy,

1983). Not surprisingly, the school culture plays a very important role in how teachers in schools respond to change efforts. Educational change efforts which have ignored the culture of the school have proven unsuccessful (Corbett and Rossman, 1989). Thus, for change to be successful, the culture of the school must be one which is supportive of change efforts.

Likewise, because the school culture is inextricably connected to the school structure, a change in the structure must be accompanied by a change in the culture, and vice versa (Hargreaves, 1994). Because traditional school practices are reinforced by the ideologies and group norms that comprise the culture of the school, it is often impossible to establish a collaborative school culture without addressing existing organizational structures. Accordingly, those who push for simply changing the structure of schools 'underestimate the traditions, assumptions, and working relationships that profoundly shape existing practice. Consequently, they also overestimate the power of structural changes to alter such practice' (Hargreaves, 1994, p. 255). For these reasons, restructuring must be accompanied by *reculturing*, as cultures are formed by and framed by specific structures (ibid.).

The role of status and power in shaping the culture of the school also runs through some of the school change literature. In *Revisiting the 'Culture of the School and the Problem of Change'*, Sarason (1996) states that in the first edition of his widely read book he

> underemphasized how power suffused all relationships in that culture: students vs. teachers, teachers vs. principals, principals vs. higher levels of administration, superintendent vs. board, the board vs. the political establishment, and that establishment vs. centers of power in the state capital. (p. 338)[1]

Sarason now asserts that 'coming to grips with the realities of the school culture requires alterations in long standing power relationships that will engender conflict and controversy' (p. 339). In many ways, by focusing on power relationships, Sarason gets to the heart of the cultural politics of school change. In fact, it is the power relationships which form the school culture that critically impact the process and progress of school change.

Competing Ideologies, Micropolitics, and Gender in School Change

Most policymakers and school change theorists imply that general change strategies, which rely on an understanding of a universal school culture, will work in any school, with any faculty, at any time, regardless of local context. The problem here is that there is not one culture that defines all schools, or even any one school. In this regard, there are several specific areas in which the school change literature falls short, perhaps because it tends to focus more generally on the process of change, rather than the actual substance of change, that is, what happens inside the 'black box' of school reform (Fullan, 1991; Huberman and Miles, 1984; Wideen, 1994). As the very title of this book suggests, school change is much messier than we think. Ideological differences, micropolitics, and gender dynamics among teachers are all part of a school's culture and, accordingly, all play into the school reform process.

The School Culture as a Site of Ideological Difference

The school culture is an ideologically contested terrain, and school change theorists do not directly deal with the ideological differences among teachers that might inhibit reculturing and/or restructuring. The literature tends to emphasize the values, norms, and habits that are held in common — the shared content of school culture, portraying culture as unitary and monolithic (see Blackmore and Kenway, 1995; Hargreaves, 1994). This oversimplified view of culture exaggerates consensus, ignoring conflict and the micropolitics of schools. In fact, the school culture itself may be the subject or site of a struggle over competing ideologies among educators, as teachers from various subcultures often have differing opinions on what to change and how to change it.

If we are to understand the political actions of teachers in reform and the various subcultures which may exist, we must delve deeper into teachers' ideologies: the beliefs teachers hold about teaching, schooling, and life in general. Teachers naturally vary in many objective dimensions, including the grade levels they teach, their subject areas, length of experience, gender, racial and ethnic background, and the type of teacher training they received; no doubt, these variations may greatly impact their ideologies and in turn their classroom practice and propensity towards reform (Sarason, 1996).[2] As research on teacher development has pointed out, efforts to change teachers' practices are always impeded by the differing values, beliefs, and assumptions that teachers hold (Nias, in press).

Critical theorists define teacher ideology in more political terms than the school change theorists, in a way that is particularly helpful for understanding the cultural politics and contested nature of local school change. Critical theorists see ideology as a set of lived meanings and practices that are often internally consistent (Apple, 1985; Giroux, 1984). Ideology can play a role in securing domination of one societal group over another. That is, teachers' ideologies are produced in the course of their interactions within the school context and the larger society in which they exist. In this way, ideologies can also operate in the service of dominant societal norms and the existing social structure (Apple, 1985). As Giroux (1984) argues, 'If we are to take human agency seriously, we must acknowledge the degree to which historical and objective social forces leave their ideological imprint on the psyche itself' (p. 318). Critical theorists stress the importance of social, political, and economic conditions around issues of race, gender, and class as shaping ideology. This wider, more explicitly political definition of ideology is important for understanding the politics of educational change.

Although gaining insight into teachers' ideologies can help make sense of their political action in reform efforts, none of the literature, with the exception of Ball (1987), has made this connection. School change theorists do not suggest strategies for change in a school culture in which ideology is contested among teachers. Since teachers' ideologies are rooted in their life experiences and interactions, teacher agency in reform is deeply embedded within a larger societal context, not just within the school. Moreover, teachers' ideologies vary as each individual teacher makes meaning of his/her world in a different way.

Yet, more generally, subcultures of teachers may share common ideologies. Teacher subcultures often share common ideologies about the purpose of education, how schools should be organized, and the role of the teacher. There are likely to be several teacher subcultures within a school depending on its history and the orientation and commitment of individuals and groups of teachers (Westoby, 1988). Subcultures may be collegial, cooperative, share a common vision, and engage in reflection and democratic decision making; or they may be quite the opposite, embodying norms of isolation and negative attitudes about schooling (McLaughlin et al., 1990).

Teacher subcultures are especially apparent in secondary schools, where the traditional organizational structure groups teachers into subject departments. However, teachers in any school may form subcultures on the basis of ideological similarities or common interests (Hargreaves, 1994; McLaughlin, 1994). For example, in their search for a self-affirmation or in the interest of achieving a greater voice in the school, teachers may group with other like-minded teachers. This can result in ideologically diverse factions or 'balkanized cultures', which may provide self-reference for individual members, but can impede whole school change efforts when they take on a political complexion (Hargreaves, 1994; Nias, in press). In addition, particular teacher sub-cultures, if collaborative, can enhance teachers' professional growth or, if balkanized, can contribute to teachers' entrenchment. Bringing such divergent groups together takes very skilled leadership and constitutes a significant, yet seldom recognized, barrier to school change (ibid.).

In sum, because change is mediated through cultures of teaching (Fullan, 1991; Sikes, 1992; Siskin, 1994), knowledge of teacher subcultures leads to a better understanding of how teachers behave politically in school reform and of the interplay of their agency with the school culture and structure. Clearly, different teacher subcultures perceive change in different ways, which in turn affects their decisions to resist or support reform efforts. More specifically, teacher subcultures play an important role in providing a source of identity for teachers and a source of political power, status, and ideological differences. Teacher subcultures can become the base of political agendas (Ball, 1987; Siskin, 1994). In a school undertaking reform, we can expect to see ideolo-gical subcultures of teachers struggling over the issue of whose defini-tion of the school will prevail. This was certainly the case in the schools discussed in this book. What is most interesting about these schools (and likely others) is that particular teacher subcultures grouped not only around common ideologies, but also, notably, around common gender, into male and female groups.

Gender and School Change

Nowhere in the current school change literature is there mention of gender. I am not the first to recognize this void (Blackmore and Kenway, 1995); however, as far as I know, this book marks the first analysis of gender in the research on school reform. The lack of attention to gender (and race and ethnicity, for that matter) is interesting, given the fact that gender can operate on the societal level as a system of power relations. In most societies, men simply have more power, controlling government, business, law, and public discourse. These social relations of power are played out on the terrain of everyday public discourse in societal institutions, including schools. Therefore, it would follow that gender would impact the process of change in most, if not all, social institutions.

While there is a dearth of literature on the intersection of gender and school reform, there is a plethora of literature on gender and teaching more generally. This research focuses on three major areas: the gendered nature of teaching as a profession (particularly at the elementary school level), the divergence of career opportunities among men and women teachers, and the counter-hegemonic, anti-sexist efforts of feminist teachers. A number of these works also discuss women teachers' lives in terms of the structural forces of patriarchy that have shaped them. This research has been very important in establishing the role of gender in structuring the professional lives of teachers, and, in the case of feminist scholarship, making women's voices and understandings the central focus of research. For these reasons, we can extract some ideas from this literature and bring them to bear on the role of gender in teacher agency in reform.

The first branch of this literature involves the gendered nature of the teaching profession, particularly at the elementary level (Apple, 1994). That is,

> particularly with elementary school teaching, the cultural construc-
> tions of teaching are so gendered, so connected with teaching defined
> as a women's activity, that it is nearly impossible to reform teaching
> without examining and confronting the gender question. (p. 5)

Traditionally, men have held administrative posts, and women, particularly in elementary schools, constitute the bulk of the teaching force. Approximately eighty-seven per cent of elementary school teachers are women; 67 per cent of teachers overall are women (Apple, 1994). Weiler's (1988) study of women teachers in two high schools suggests that the gender question is not unique to the elementary school setting. In fact, in her analysis of women teachers' lives, Weiler concludes that the female secondary school teachers are strongly influenced by hegemonic ideology (particularly that of sexism) and by material structures.

Based on this literature, I have several hypotheses for how the gendered nature of the teaching profession might affect teachers in reform. First, we might expect that reforms, particularly at the secondary level, that ask teachers to do what could be construed as 'women's work' would likely meet resistance from men. For example, many of the current middle school reforms (which propose homerooms, advisory periods, and self-contained classes), aimed at improving the transition for children from elementary to high school, might be perceived negatively by male teachers. Second, if, as Weiler (1988) suggests, women teachers experience sexism in their jobs at all levels, we can expect that sexism would play a role in shaping discussions among teachers grappling with reform. The contributions by women teachers may be perceived as less important, simply by virtue of their gender.

The second branch of literature on gender and teaching involves gender differences in the careers of teachers (see Acker, 1989, for a comprehensive review). The career opportunities of men and women teachers sharply diverge. There are gender differences in subjects taught by men and women and in administrative responsibilities of men and women teachers (Acker, 1989). Men and women teachers still do not hold an equal number of promoted positions (Ridell, 1989). Historical analyses of the teaching profession suggest that the use of gender stereotypes for the social control of women teachers began very early in the history of American education (Casey and Apple, 1989). Even as recently as the 1970s, researchers implicated women teachers for their lack of commitment to the profession and their predeliction to take time off for their families (Dreeben, 1970; Lortie, 1975).

Ridell (1989) found that male teachers whom she interviewed accepted uncritically that when women teachers made the choice to have children, they were exhibiting a lack of interest in their teaching careers. Moreover, because their teaching careers are often looked upon as secondary to their duties as wives and a mothers, women teachers are often passed over for promotions to administrative positions (Sikes et al., 1985). These assumptions about women teachers serve to justify gender inequalites and conceal the structural forces shaping these teachers' lives. Grant (1989), in a critique of these stereotypical beliefs about women teachers, argues that given traditional role expectations and responsibilities in society, it is inappropriate to expect most women to adopt a single-minded approach to career advancement. Rather, there are different periods in women's lives when they might be more or less career driven. For example, Sikes et al.'s (1985) qualitative study of teacher careers found that women teachers often pursue promotion and greater responsibility after age forty when their families are no longer as dependent upon them.

The common assumptions about women teachers' apparent lack of interest in their careers are curious in light of research that shows that women teachers are more likely than men teachers to say they have always wanted to teach (Shakeshaft and Perry, 1995). Men teachers are more likely to have gotten into teaching by accident or as a second choice (ibid.). However, despite these findings, in reality the careers of women and men teachers are looked upon quite differently, and this too may impact their role in reform. For example, one might imagine a school change scenario in which women teachers over age forty, choosing to now invest more time into their careers, may spearhead a reform movement at their school. Yet, these women teachers may not be taken seriously by veteran male teachers in their school who know that these same teachers took time off several years before to raise their children.

The third branch of literature on gender and teaching focuses on women teachers who are working for social change or advancing a feminist pedagogy through their attempts to enlighten female students (Blackmore and Kenway, 1995; Casey, 1993; Weiler, 1988). Casey (1993), drawing on Gramsci's (1971) work on social change, uses life history, oral history, and discourse analysis to illuminate the narratives of politically progressive women teachers. Weiler (1988) blends together critical theory and feminist theory in a study of the counter-hegemonic practices of feminist high school teachers. Blackmore and Kenway (1995) discuss the efforts of women teachers who are helping to liberate female students by making 'resistant discourses and subject positions more widely available' (p. 247).

The research on women teachers working for social change has obvious applications for school reform. First, we gain an understanding of some of the barriers women teachers face in challenging patriarchal school cultures. However, past research has mostly looked at the reform efforts of these teachers working in isolation, in the context of their classrooms, and not in a broader, school-wide arena. Thus, we have little knowledge of what might happen if a group of women teachers were to launch a school-wide change effort which affects men and women teachers alike.

Finally, while we are just beginning to hear the voices of women teachers in the literature, there is more substantial literature on the feminist attributes of leadership or, generally, women in educational administration (e.g., Regan and Brooks, 1995; Restine, 1993; Shakeshaft and Perry, 1995). This research focuses on the qualities that women bring to leadership that are inherently different from those brought by men, and on the differences in administrative styles of men and women administrators. Women administrators are portrayed as more caring, better listeners, and more faciliatory than men in their interactions with teachers — all characteristics learned through socialization. Drawing from this literature, we might expect to see gender-specific styles of interaction in how men and women teachers negotiate reform with each other in their schools. Or, we might see different leadership styles among men and women teachers spearheading reform movements.

In sum, the plethora of literature on gender and teaching suggests that gender is a strong shaping principle of social differentiation in the lives of teachers. This literature helps us better understand how gender might impact school reform, a perspective which is sorely needed given the dearth of school change literature on this topic. After all, social differentiation is suffused by power differentiation and, therefore, it is likely that social structures such as gender shape and are shaped by teachers' interactions in reform.

The Micropolitics of School Change

While the school change literature does address the problem of hierarchical power relations in inhibiting reform (Sarason, 1996), it does not focus on the need to alter relations of power between teachers. Differential power relations between teachers at a school may be related to past histories (old guard vs. new guard), administrator preferences, or departmental affiliations. Or, most importantly, teachers may come to the school reform process from different social locations (e.g., gender, race, ethnic backgrounds), and this positionality impacts their role in the politics of school reform, as some social locations (men vs. women) enjoy a more privileged status.

What I am referring to here is school micropolitics, which is something the school change research tends to ignore (see Hargreaves et al., 1996) Yet, I am suggesting a wider view of micropolitics which includes and even emphasizes the impact of social relations of power in shaping the micropolitics of schools. In the introduction to this book, I argued that school change can become a micropolitical battle focused on adult agendas in which the core issues of teaching and learning fall into the background. Here, I discuss research on the micropolitics of education, which does not specifically focus on school change or on the dynamics of social relations, but provides a helpful way of understanding the key issues in the politics of reform.

Why use a micropolitical perspective? Several explanations are offered. First, organizational theory tells us little about daily life in schools and tends to emphasize shared goals, consensus, and similarity. Conversely, micropolitical analysis emphasizes power, ideological diversity, and political action (Ball, 1987). Also, by studying micropolitics, we can gain an understanding of how and why certain individuals and groups can shape what happens in schools through their power and dominance over others.

Research on the micropolitics of education is concerned with conflict between different interest groups in school communities, focusing specifically on how such political phenomena affect schools (Iannaccone, 1991; Marshall and Scribner 1991). These competing interests, ideologies, and the informal negotiations of turf in schools are the essence of micropolitics:

> Micropolitics is the nexus where the formal structure of roles interpenetrates with the informal pattern of influence. It is a skill of judgment and coalition building rather than position. Thus power is a goal, an outcome, rather than a precondition of political process. It is also a career, a vehicle, a channel. For some it is a way of life, an end in itself. It is what they do . . . It is perhaps a macho, masculine preoccupation, boys' games. (Ball, 1987, p. 246)

Similarly, Hoyle (1986) describes micropolitics as the 'organizational underworld' that we know very little about because it is 'almost a taboo subject in "serious" discussion, yet informally it is a favorite theme of organizational gossip as people talk about "playing politics", "hidden agendas", "organizational mafias", "Machiavellianism" and so forth . . .' (p. 125). What is common to both Ball's and Hoyle's descriptions of micropolitics are the elements of subversiveness and seediness in micropolitics; it is therefore not surprising that most studies of school change do not address it. In fact, collecting data on school micropolitics is often difficult, as it requires digging deep into issues about which school personnel may not be very forthcoming, often for fear of the consequences if they discuss such issues publicly.

Micropolitics of the school is a relatively new area of study, and we are still unsure as to where micropolitics fits in the context of social theory or how the boundaries of the field are defined. Until recently, much research has been focused on the politics outside school; little research focuses on how people within schools exercise power, the manner in which particular contexts impact their ability to influence policy or practice, and even less on the political strategies that teachers employ (Blase, 1989; Malen, 1995).

Nevertheless, there is a small but growing body of research studies on the micropolitics of education which help to unravel the realities of school life by showing how the politics in and around schools affect how schools manage educational issues. Much of the research in the area of micropolitics of the school focuses on hierarchical relationships that exist within the school (Iannaccone, 1991). Blase (1989; 1993) has contributed a number of important works in this area, probing into teachers' political orientations vis-à-vis the principal. Malen and Ogawa (1988) investigate the political role of parents on school site councils. Despite this wide scope, very little research focuses on teacher-teacher political orientations. Ball (1987) is a notable exception.

Perhaps the most applicable work on the micropolitics and school reform, as it relates to teachers, is Ball's (1987), *The Micro-politics of the School: Towards a Theory of School Organization*. To illustrate the micropolitical perspective, Ball relies on qualitative data from a variety of studies, including a case study of 'Beachside' comprehensive school, where heterogeneous grouping was introduced. Ball found that reform was characterized by an opposition between contrasting definitions of the comprehensive school: one emphasizing access and the other outcomes. These contrasting definitions were associated with competing educational ideologies, and the subtext of the argument was concerned with a broader and longer term struggle for power and influence within the school.

A study by Noblit, Berry, and Demsey (1991) also assesses teachers' political responses to reform. In a rather cynical statement, the authors remark that 'at a minimum, reform is an opportunity for political action. At most, the meaning of reform is what the teachers decide to make of it' (p. 380). In a comparative case study of two elementary schools, the authors assess the teachers' response to a district-established career development program, finding that although the district attempted to create a structure to overcome the lack of shared beliefs among teachers, they achieved the unanticipated outcome of increased teacher political power. This study makes an important contribution by highlighting the salience of micropolitics in reform; however, its focus is on top-down change and not on locally developed change, as discussed in this book.

The micropolitical perspective reminds us that school reform is rarely a politically neutral event; some even argue that reforms enter schools already politically organized (Noblit et al., 1991). It also reminds us that schools are as much a venue for adult-adult relationships, as they are for teaching and learning (Nias, in press). Because reform is rarely politically neutral, and because of the fact that teachers often have one overriding concern — the preservation of a stable sense of personal and professional identities (ibid.) — reforms often provoke factionalism in schools on various lines including departmental, old guard vs. new guard, race, and, in this case, gender. In terms of gender, the micropolitical perspective suggests that 'the roots of [women's] inaction may lie in their relatively powerless structural position in the mixed secondary school, rather than their simply being women' (Acker, 1994, p. 101).

Thus far, very few studies of micropolitics have looked at the ways in which gender or, more generally, social relations of power impact the micropolitics of schools. In fact, Ball (1987) states that one of the risks in micropolitical analysis is to downplay the role of structural features in organizing everyday life and overemphasize internal factors. Further work needs to be done in relating the external elements of the school environment to the internal political behaviors (Blase,

1993; Iannaccone, 1991). This book hopes to add insight into how social relations of gender impact the micropolitics of reform.

The aforementioned literature on micropolitics leaves us wanting for a way of making sense of how hostilities between opposing groups, with different ideologies and goals, might be expressed in the context of school reform. Just how might we expect the struggle for or against reform to play itself out among teachers? How do we make sure to attend to gender and other wider social relations of power? I find the *politics of representation* serves as a helpful organizing framework.

The Politics of Representation

The politics of representation is the competition that takes place among individuals or factions over the meaning of ambiguous events, people, and objects in the world. The way in which events, objects, or people are represented in discourse gives them a particular meaning (Mehan, 1993). Representations do not mimic reality, but rather are the medium through which things take on meaning and value (Shapiro, 1987). There is often competition over the appropriate or correct way of representing social facts, objects, or people, as proponents of various positions attempt to dominate modes of representation. This is accomplished by advocates of a particular position in a variety of ways, including persuading others to join their side, coopting the opposition's discourse, and silencing the opponents by attacking them:

> If successful, a hierarchy is formed, in which one mode of representing the world gains primacy over others, transforming modes of representation from an array on a horizontal plane to a ranking on a vertical plane. (Mehan, 1993; p. 241)

Discourse, and its accompanying political or social action, does not necessarily happen only in the context of a conversation between two or more individuals. Rather, public political discourse exists, resembling a quasi-conversation between voices which represent institutional viewpoints. That is, voices in interaction mutually influence each other and reciprocally react to one another (Mehan, Nathanson and Skelly, 1990).

Modes of representing events differ according to a person's social location: Speech is constituted by the history of a person's place in gender, class, race, and institutional arrangements. Groups or individuals can have profoundly different meanings of the same situation, depending on their ideologies, belief systems, or experiences. This is true of teachers in schools who may view a reform as either an opportunity or as a major hindrance. However, not all definitions are equally valid. In an unequal power situation, more powerful groups or individuals can impose their definition of a situation on others (Mehan, 1990). This has striking consequences for teachers in schools as not all teachers have equal power. Sometimes these power differences overlap with gender.

The connection between power and discourse inherent in the politics of representation emerges from a constitutive theory of human action. A constitutive theory treats language as an active political force composed of practices which define the objects of which they speak (Mehan, Nathanson and Skelly, 1990). Mead (1934) reminds us that 'language is never arbitrary in the sense of simply denoting a bare state of consciousness by a word' (p. 75). Language is part of the social process; it is how we mediate a social situation and how political action is sometimes achieved. Pertaining to schools, a constitutive theory of action asks how the stable features of schools are generated in and revealed by the institution's participants (Mehan, 1993).[3]

What is key to the politics of representation is the inextricable connection between language and power. The connection between language and power is linked to the theoretical perspectives of the more recent post-modernism and critical theory (e.g., Foucault, 1984) and finds its roots in social constructionist theories (e.g., Berger and Luckmann, 1967). The overarching theme here is 'the more powerful the people, the larger their verbal possibilities in discourse' (Wodak, 1995, p. 33).

Power is often expressed through the use of language and symbols in the micropolitics of the school. The strategic use of discourse is among the most influential micropolitical processes. More powerful groups can use language to define what questions and issues are seen as important in the setting (such as whether or not reform is necessary), rendering the definitions held by less powerful groups seemingly irrational (Berger and Luckmann, 1967; Corson, 1995; Marshall and Scribner, 1991). In sum, groups use language as a vehicle to socially construct reality and manipulate power relations.

The language-power link is also key for this study as ideology is often represented as talk (Labov, 1990). When people describe issues or situations, ideological themes are often reflected. The issues then become under what circumstances do ideologies come to be defined as dominant, and whose ideology predominates. For example, school reform is often an ideological battle among competing interest groups, and this battle is manifested through discourse.

The connection between language and power is also evident in gender studies, and it is here that we can see the influence of social location on the politics of representation. Feminist researchers, both in education and more broadly, see gender relations as constructed through the discourse of organizations (Biklen, 1995; Blackmore and Kenway, 1995; Casey, 1993; Gherardi, 1995; Mann, 1994; Uchida, 1992). Gender, argues Crawford (1995), is what the culture makes of the dichotomy of sex. In other words, gender is in part a social construct that evolves from how males and females are treated differently in our patriarchal society and is produced in the course of interaction and discourse (Uchida, 1992). As Gherardi (1995) explains, 'how gender is 'done' in an organization is a crucial cultural phenomenon' and is a central question of the micropolitics between men and women (p. 4).

Similarly, feminist researchers in education argue that gender relations within schools are not merely a pale reflection of gender relations in the society, but rather that people construct gender in the course of their interactions, many of which are verbal (Biklen, 1995; Casey, 1993). For example, various studies on interactional norms in conversation have shown that men are able to exert control over topics and themes (Ball, 1987). Men may exert their dominance by finishing women's sentences, interrupting without permission, or not responding to women's comments. Women, on the other hand, are typically supportive and faciliatory when interacting with men in a discussion, surrendering control to them. Additionally, in schools, where women have established the right to participate in decision making, they often find themselves in a double-bind: 'If individual women or groups do attempt to assert themselves in discussions or meetings, they are liable to find themselves labeled by men as aggressive, loud mouthed, or essentially unfeminine' (Ball, 1987, p. 77).

In looking into the different ways in which people represent events or objects through language, gender plays an important role. We tend to think of women's ways of talking as being endemic to their biological makeup as women, as separate from their interactions and experiences (Gray, 1992; Lakoff and Johnson, 1975).[4] This obfuscates the issue, treating language as a sex-based trait, rather than a product of gender-based interactions. Men and women behave in gendered ways because they exist in gendered social contexts (Crawford, 1995; Uchida, 1992). The relationship between gender and language should be approached from the viewpoint that we are 'doing gender' in interaction (Uchida, 1992). In sum, males often dominate women in discourse as their social interaction occurs within the context of a patriarchal society. However, while social location is often determinant of power relations in discourse,

> To understand how gender relations are played out in talk, we would need to analyze talk within its local context (i.e., the relative power and status of each participant, the salience of gender in the situation), its larger context (the speech communities in which the speakers function) and the cultural constructions of gender that inform it. (Crawford, 1995, p. 45)

In other words, organizations also vary in how their discourse shapes gender relations. Organizations are constrained and shaped by the grammar of the social structure, but they are also constituted by — and constitute — the discourse practices that occur within them. It follows that not all organizations are alike — some organizational cultures are more or less 'women-friendly', and, likewise, 'the structuring of gender varies among organizations' and may vary within organizations at different times and in different settings in an organization (Gherardi, 1995, p. 16).

This distinction is key for understanding the gender discourse among men and women teachers in school settings. A school may be more or less 'women-friendly' and the organizational culture and the discourse around gender may vary over time, depending on the actors involved and the particular circumstances. This will become more clear in Chapter 5 as I contrast the gender politics at Central to the gender politics at two other schools, Explorer and Grant.

Conclusion

What I have attempted to show in this review of the literature is that the relationship between gender politics and educational change can best be understood in the context of a framework that regards language as constitutive of political phenomena, rather than simply about political phenomena. Bringing issues from the literature on school change, gender, and micropolitics into conversation with qualitative data from a school in which gender politics emerged as a shaping force in the reform is a powerful way to investigate how teachers struggle to redefine what 'school' means.

In the subsequent chapters, I investigate the politics of representation concerning the two chief factions of teachers at Central High School — The Idea Team and the Good Old Boys. Specifically, I focus on the conventions and discourse strategies that are revealed in the contest over meaning among these gender-based factions. At Central, one of the ways in which the faction of male teachers dominates is by shifting from a discourse of education to a discourse of gender politics.

Notes

1 Without detracting from Sarason's important list of power relations, note that the teacher-teacher relationship, which is the touchstone of this entire book, is not included. I raise this shortly in my section on power and micropolitics.

2 Researchers have looked at how teachers' ideologies affect their classroom practices (Anyon, 1981; Metz, 1978; McLaughlin and Talbert, 1993), finding that teachers' receptiveness to undertaking teaching strategies that emphasize complex tasks and critical thinking is influenced by what they believe are appropriate strategies for teaching students of a particular social class. Similarly, Anyon's (1981) study of instruction in five schools serving families of varying social class also showed that teachers had varying educational goals and used differential teaching strategies depending on the social class background of the students in their school. These findings serve as a reminder that 'policy coherence as intended by reformers and policy makers ultimately is achieved or denied in the subjective responses of teachers — in teachers' social construction of students' (McLaughlin and Talbert, 1993, p. 248). Here we also see the ways in which historical and social forces are imprinted in the ideologies of teachers and how this impacts their classroom interactions.

3 Mehan (1993) investigated the politics of representation in a case study of how a student's classification as 'learning disabled' is constructed in the course of interaction between educators and parents. He found that the professional educators' representation of the student overrode the parents' representation, concluding that institutionally grounded representations predominate. Educators reproduced the status relations among the different discourses that exist in society.

4 As Crawford (1995) points out, much of this research treats men and women as fundamentally different in terms of personality, beliefs, and goals before they even enter conversation, and accordingly it is not surprising that they talk differently as well. The difference schema connects to common wisdom about men and women that is endorsed by the mass media and the dominant culture. For women, different often means deficient. This 'difference' framework is contrasted with the research discussed here that focuses on male dominance and the sexual division of labor in talk (Uchida, 1992).

2   Central High School:
The Case and its Context

This chapter sets the stage for the rest of the book, beginning with a description of the case study methodology used in this study. The significance of *detracking*, a major component of Central High School's restructuring plan, is also considered. What follows is a discussion of Central High School and its context, including the demographics of the school, district, and community, and a description of the larger economic, political, and social conditions around reform at Central. Finally, this chapter includes a summary of the key events in reform at Central High School.

The *Beyond Sorting and Stratification* Study

The data for this book was collected as part of a larger comparative case study of ten racially mixed secondary schools undertaking alternatives to tracking. Building on prior research on tracking and desegregation by the project directors (Oakes, 1985; Wells, 1991), the *Beyond Sorting and Stratification* study examined the technical aspects of detracking reforms as well as the normative and political issues inherent in the school change process (Oakes and Wells, 1996; Oakes et al., 1997; Wells and Serna, 1996).

The *Beyond Sorting and Stratification* study grew out of an interest in discovering some of the ways in which racially-mixed schools were moving away from tracking. Tracking, almost universal in American schools for the past century, is the practice of sorting students into different programs of study based on their perceived academic ability. The term 'tracking' is often used interchangeably with the terms 'ability grouping', 'homogeneous grouping', and 'curriculum differentiation'. These terms all imply some means of grouping students for instruction by ability or achievement in order to create homogeneous instructional groups. Ability grouping at the elementary level usually leads to tracking at the secondary level. Secondary schools vary in the number, size, and composition of tracks; however, students are generally assigned to a track level — basic, regular, college preparatory, or honors/ advanced placement — in which they remain for their high school career.

The most disturbing finding about tracking is the strong correlation between race, social class, and track placement. Studies consistently find that low income and minority students are disproportionately placed in low track classes, and advantaged and white students are more often placed in the high track (Braddock and Dawkins, 1993; Oakes, 1985). In high schools, low income, African-American, and Latino students are underrepresented in college preparatory programs, and they are more frequently enrolled in vocational programs that train for low-paying, dead-end jobs (Oakes, 1987). At all levels, minority students lack representation in programs for gifted and talented students. However, despite extensive research suggesting that track placement is influenced by race and social class biases, proponents believe that tracking is meritocratic. Furthermore, many educators strongly believe that students learn better in groups with other students like themselves (Kulik and Kulik, 1982).

Research has consistently shown that when schools track, students from different racial groups are not offered equal opportunities to learn (Oakes, 1985; Oakes, Gamoran and Page, 1992). African-American and Latino students who are disproportionately placed in low track classes systematically receive fewer resources: teachers are less qualified, expectations are lower, the curriculum is watered down, and there are fewer classroom materials. White students who are disproportionately placed in the high track are advantaged by receiving more qualified teachers, greater classroom resources, and an enriched curriculum designed to prepare them to attend college (Oakes, Gamoran and Page, 1992). As a result, tracking leads to class- and race-linked differences in opportunities to learn and gaps in achievement between white students and their minority peers. Additionally, because tracking in racially mixed schools resegregates students, it constrains inter-group relations and perpetuates stereotypes related to race (Oakes and Wells, 1995).

The negative research findings on tracking and the increased attention from civil rights groups, such as the ACLU, who view tracking as the most important 'second generation' desegregation issue, have led policymakers to consider alternatives to tracking (Oakes and Wells, 1996; Welner and Oakes, 1996). Educators across the country have begun to experiment with detracking in their schools. We conducted the *Beyond Sorting and Stratification* study in order to learn more about the detracking efforts of some of these educators. We wanted to know how detracking came about in their schools and what strategies they used to reorganize their schools and revamp curriculum and instruction. We also wanted to understand how educators implemented their plans, what barriers they faced, and what facilitated their detracking efforts. Finally, we wanted to know how various groups — educators, parents, students, and community members — responded to detracking (Oakes and Wells, 1995).

The principal investigators of this study were Professors Jeannie Oakes and Amy Stuart Wells at the UCLA Graduate School of Education.[1] The study was staffed by eight research associates, including myself, making up a research team which was racially, ethnically, age, and gender diverse.[2] The members of our team also represented a variety of disciplinary perspectives and work experiences in the field of education.

There were six high schools and four middle schools in the *Beyond Sorting and Stratification* study. Central High School, the primary focus of this book, was one of the high schools, and the two schools described in Chapter 5, Explorer Middle School and Grant High School, were also part of the study. All ten schools were racially mixed and were at different stages in their implementation of detracking reforms. They were located in various geographic regions of the country and were situated in urban, suburban, and rural areas.

Case study methodology was chosen for the detracking study because it is a method which enabled us to examine the process and consequences of school changes in the real life contexts in which they occurred (Yin, 1989). Since the schools in the detracking study were at various stages in the process of implementing alternatives to tracking, we were able to document educators' reform efforts as they were taking place. Thus, case study methodology allowed for an in-depth study of how policy decisions played out in local-level school contexts (Darling-Hammond, 1990).

The detracking study was designed to be longitudinal because we expected that the comprehensive nature of significant tracking alternatives would require a long and slow change process. Each school was assigned one researcher who took primary responsibility for that school throughout the study. As the primary researcher for Central High School, I made four visits to the school, with each visit lasting three to five full days. The visits to Central High School took place in November 1992, March 1993, May 1994, and finally, June 1996. During each visit from 1992 to 1994, I was accompanied by one or more researchers on our team. This allowed for continuity across site visits while adding the varied perspective of another researcher who had visited various other schools in our study.

In order to closely monitor the school change process, I had ample phone contact and several follow-up meetings with administrators and teachers at Central. In August 1995, I circulated a lengthy case report to five people at the school for feedback. These people were chosen because they represented diverse view points on the issue of reform at the school. In addition, in June 1996, I returned to the school and conducted fifteen interviews with teachers and administrators in order to further validate our findings and to get a sense of what had changed in the school over the past two years.[3]

We collected data through a variety of means including interviews, classroom and meeting observations, and school and community documents. We felt that these diverse sources would not only help us triangulate our findings (Yin, 1989), but would also help us look closely at the three dimensions — technical, normative, and political — that guided the theoretical framework of this study of detracking from the beginning (Oakes and Wells, 1995).

We also looked for evidence that detracking was part of a larger plan to change the curriculum and instructional practices at the school because research reveals that tracking co-exists with many problematic school practices (Oakes and Lipton, 1992). We were also guided by the belief that while new technologies and organizational arrangements are necessary for detracking, they must make sense to educators before they can be implemented (ibid.). Because tracking is held in place by beliefs that the American educational system is meritocratic, we also expected that a redistributive policy like detracking would likely make those who benefit from a privileged position in the status quo rather uneasy. Moreover, since detracking asks teachers to confront powerful societal conceptions of ability that relate to race and class, we attempted to gain insight into teachers' ideologies about such issues (Oakes and Wells, 1996). To do this, we had to delve deeply into these political dimensions of detracking reform (Oakes et al., 1997).

To gather data on all of these issues, we conducted extensive interviews with people who represented stakeholders in detracking reform, including teachers, parents and community members, students, and school and district administrators. For example, during each regularly scheduled visit to Central High School, our research team conducted an average of thirty-five to forty interviews. We interviewed forty-five of the eighty-one teachers on the faculty. We interviewed teachers who were particularly good informants two or three times. The interviewed teachers represented a diversity of departments, factions, ages, ethnic and racial backgrounds, length of time at the school, and involvement level in the reform. We also conducted numerous lengthy interviews with the principal, assistant principals, and the assistant superintendent. We interviewed the superintendent, two of the five school board members, five counselors, fifteen students, and seven parents. We made formal observations of thirty classes, twelve school meetings, and collected many school and district documents relevant to both the school context and the reform efforts taking place.

The data collection efforts at the two detracking schools, Explorer Middle School and Grant High School, discussed in Chapter 5 followed the same schedule and research protocol as the data collection efforts at Central. At all schools, we used semi-structured interview protocols, asking open-ended questions of respondents (see Appendix). Teachers were asked about their involvement in the change efforts going on at their schools. We asked teachers about what helped or hindered their reform efforts and what they had learned about school change. Initially, some teachers were reluctant to talk with us, fearing that we would report their opinions back to other staff. Over time, however, as teachers realized that their identities were held in confidence, they became more open. Many seemed to view their interviews with us as a cathartic experience, as it gave them the opportunity to talk with outsiders about the trials and tribulations of reform at their school. Interviews lasted an average of forty-five minutes to one hour, although many were longer. All of these interviews were taped and transcribed at the completion of each school site visit.

We spent a disproportionate amount of our time in the field interviewing teachers, as teachers play a very important role in tracking and detracking. In particular, research has shown that teachers are active agents in creating and sustaining tracking (Finley, 1984; Oakes, 1985; Oakes, Gamoran and Page, 1992).[4] In most schools, teachers are responsible for recommending appropriate track placement for their students. Additionally, studies consistently find that teachers have very different goals and expectations for students in different tracks. Teachers of low ability classes place less emphasis on subject-related curriculum goals. On the other hand, teachers expect that high track students become interested in the subject matter, acquire basic concepts and principles, and develop inquiry approaches and problem solving techniques. These goals are typically seen as less important for low track students (Oakes, Gamoran and Page, 1992). Teachers also sustain tracking by actively competing among themselves for the high track classes within a school, which are often seen by teachers as rewards (Finley, 1984).[5] Finally, teacher tracking is most likely in schools with racially diverse student populations and faculties and least likely in schools serving a mostly white, high income population (Talbert and Ennis, 1990).

Accordingly, we expected that because teachers are often actors in creating and sustaining tracking, they must also be recognized as active agents in detracking. Detracking is hard work for teachers. While detracking will most likely make teachers' jobs more interesting, detracking also makes teaching more difficult, at least initially, requiring the creativity and willingness to learn and try new methods of instruction (Oakes and Lipton, 1992). Teachers also need to expand their knowledge in order to teach a wider range of students (O'Neil, 1993). Furthermore, the school environment must be one that allows teachers to try new ideas. Detracking also requires new professional relationships among teachers. In some schools undertaking detracking, teachers at the secondary level are no longer grouped by subject, but rather they teach in interdisciplinary teams (Common Destiny Alliance, 1992). Most importantly, prior research suggested that a detracking effort will fail without the support of teachers (Common Destiny Alliance, 1992; Oakes and Lipton, 1992). Therefore, we sought to understand the teachers' roles as supporters or resisters of reform.

Teachers in favor of detracking often have to defend their beliefs within a larger structure and culture which may not be supportive of such goals (Oakes and Wells, 1996). Detracking also changes the distribution of power and privilege among teachers, often leading to a struggle to preserve the status quo on the part of those teachers who had previously benefited from the track structure, as was the case at Central and Grant.

In summary, the data used for this book includes thousands of pages of transcribed interviews with school personnel and district personnel, interviews with parents and students, documents describing the schools' reform efforts, observations, and field notes. In this book I have also relied upon case reports that had been prepared for each school (Datnow, 1995; Hirshberg, 1995; Ray, 1995). Using methods detailed by Miles and Huberman (1984), Yin (1989), and Strauss and Corbin (1990), in the process of analysis, I have brought the data collected in the detracking study into an on-going conversation with a theoretical framework that brought together literature in education, gender studies, sociology, political science, and anthropology.

Since Central High School represents the major focus of this book, I now turn to an overview of the reform efforts that took place at the school over the several years during which data was collected. The significance of detracking in Central High School's reform efforts is evident in the following discussion and in the subsequent chapters. Moreover, at Central, the agency of teachers had much to do with the fact that detracking was a politically loaded reform, about which educators have very strong, often divergent, beliefs.

A Profile of Central High School

School Demographics

Central High School is located in an agricultural community in the western United States. The city of Central has a population of approximately 150,000 residents, many of whom are involved in the local farming industry. The city is characterized by residential segregation; most notably, white, upper income families live in suburban communities and in the city's affluent riverside area, and low-income Latino families live in the local 'barrio' or in temporary housing structures near farming areas. The small African-American population is scattered throughout middle class communities in the city. The Central community was growing as families relocated from nearby congested urban areas, and tourism in the city was increasing as new hotels were built along the riverside.

Central High School was situated in the center of the city, surrounded by several residential blocks, the city's community center and municipal buildings, and retail establishments. The school campus was a cluster of long one-story buildings; classrooms were spread out in rows, connected by outdoor corridors. In the center of the campus there was an open quadrangle where students congregated at lunch. In general, the physical plant was in bad repair. However, there was little or no visible graffiti, as the administration directed that it be painted over each morning.[6]

During the period of the study, Central was a naturally mixed neighborhood school with 2200 students, grades nine through twelve. Central was characterized by considerable diversity among its student population. The racial and ethnic breakdown of the student body was 62 per cent Latino, 23 per cent white, six per cent African-American, 4 per cent Filipino, 3 per cent Asian-American, 1 per cent Pacific Islander, and 1 per cent Native American. Over the preceding ten years, the Latino and non-native English speaking population had increased dramatically, while the white population had steadily decreased. Of the Latino population, the majority were of Mexican descent, although a portion were from Guatemala and El Salvador. Most notably, 45 per cent of Central's students were classified as Limited English Proficient. The school had a bi-modal socioeconomic distribution; most of the Latino students were from low-income families, and most of the white students were from upper-middle class families.

Central's staff included eighty-one teachers, five full-time counselors, one nurse, one school psychologist, a principal, and two assistant principals. Of the teachers, 42 per cent held masters degrees, and the majority were teaching in their major field of preparation. The Central teaching staff was quite experienced: 38 per cent had more than twenty years of service, 43 per cent had ten to twenty years of service, 14 per cent had five to nine years of service, and only 5 per cent of the teachers had taught for fewer than five years. About 75 per cent of the teachers were white, while approximately 10 per cent were Latino; African-American and Asian-American teachers made up the smallest percentage, with only two or three teachers of each ethnicity. Of the eighty-one teachers who were on the faculty, forty-four were male and thirty-seven were female.

The Reputation of the School

Historically, Central High School was known to be a school with low academic standards. As a district administrator stated, 'It is not a college preparatory school'. Central had a reputation in the community as a 'tough school' fraught with violence and gang problems. Some community members called this an 'undeserved negative reputation' due mostly to bad press by local papers. However, by most measures and by comparison to other schools in the district, Central did not boast a stellar academic record. In 1992, Central was sending only 10 to 12 per cent of its graduates on to four year colleges, the majority of whom were white. Tracking was extensive, with a minimum of three tracks existing in each department, and minority students were disproportionately placed in non-college preparatory tracks.

Central's history was also distinguished by considerable turnover in the administrative staff: the school had seven principals over the preceding twenty years. When our data collection at the school began in 1992, the staff included an enthusiastic principal, Bob Foster, who had been at the school for only one year; a reform-minded assistant principal, Betty Allen, who had been at the school for four years; and Tom Baxter, an assistant principal, who had been at the school for over twenty years. Many teachers agreed that Bob Foster's leadership was the strongest that they had on the campus in many years.

The District and Community Context

Central High School is one of five schools in a union high school district. Central was known as the 'mother' school because it was the first high school in the city. Within the district, Central was among several schools with a high Latino population and low to average student achievement levels. District and school officials greatly feared white flight from Central to a whiter and wealthier school in the district, as a set of new state laws allowed both intra- and inter-district student transfers based on parental choice. Flight to private schools was not a threat, as the vast majority of school-age children in the city of Central attended public schools.

While Central did not have a very favorable academic reputation, there were many long-time community residents, including many alumni of Central High, who strongly supported the school's athletic activities. One parent remarked that at a Parent Teacher Association (PTA) dinner honoring alumni service award recipients, 'a few of the alumni brought in their old high school sweaters. One lady had it from Central High School from 1959. That's where they graduated from, and they still want to keep the sweaters'. In this regard, Central High School was viewed as a fixture in the community — many residents clung to the Central High School of yesteryear.

The local political climate at Central was one in which a small white power group was slowly being challenged by politically active Latinos and African-Americans. Local power in the city of Central had traditionally been based in a small group of powerful whites. These local power elites had been in the city a long time and were described as 'old land families' in this agricultural area. Administrators at Central believed, however, that there was a slight shift in power toward minority populations. This recent phenomena was evidenced by the election of a Latino mayor and an African-American city councilperson for the first time. According to long-time residents of the community, although minorities had more control of local politics than ever, they still posed little threat to the small white power elite.

The school's Parent Teacher Association (PTA) also represented a powerful constituency in the school community. A district office administrator credited the PTA with the 'power to make or break principals' by lobbying the school board for or against them. The PTA was mostly composed of affluent white parents and several middle class African-American parents. Very few Latino parents were represented on the PTA. The teachers' union was another powerful group in influencing school and district policy making. Relations between the union and the district were generally good, and the district office had weekly consultations with the local union leadership. The union was perceived as very strong in the district and was successful in securing a contract that provided teachers with higher salaries than in any of the neighboring districts. The union had a powerful presence at Central, as the union president, Bill Dalton, who had run unopposed four times, was a math teacher on the faculty. The strength of the union was also recognized within the school. As assistant principal Tom Baxter stated, 'We have a very strong union. The union has brought in the idea that they're running the school'. We will see the influence of the union and its president in the process of reform in Chapter 4.

The district school board, elected at-large also represented a powerful force. The five members of the board included four white professionals (3 females, 1 male) from the most affluent part of the city who had served on the board for some time, and an African-American male who was newly elected to the school board. The white male on the school board, Bill Bathgate, was a former teacher and administrator (principal) at Central High School and represented a very powerful political force in the Central community. As a former principal at Central, he maintained strong ties to teachers at the school. A parent explained Mr Bathgate's strong presence at Central: '[Mr Bathgate] comes on to campus without even coming through the front office. . . . He goes and talks to these teachers, his old cronies'. Mr Bathgate had an unusual political history in the district: as Central's principal, he was fired by the former superintendent. He subsequently ran for the school board, won, and proceeded to fire the superintendent who fired him. He was known for being able to sway the votes of other board members, and was a close friend of the current superintendent, Rich Beaufort, whom he hired while on the board. Rumor had it that Bathgate and Beaufort played golf together on a regular basis.

The school board was divided on the issue of school reform. As it turned out, the African-American man and one of the white women were the only two board members who favored Central High School's reform efforts. The remaining members, including Bill Bathgate, who constituted the voting majority, were much more circumspect about reform. Overall, the school board still reflected the fact that a white power elite in Central controlled local politics.

As the rest of this book illustrates, understanding the local context of Central High School is important because many of the struggles educators faced at the school level were reflective of political, social, and economical forces outside the school. Of course, this is true for most schools, being social institutions; however, with Central, the boundaries between the school and its context became particularly blurred, as this was a relatively small community with active local politics and strong community leaders. We will see how these contextual forces play out as the description of the change process unfolds in the following two chapters.

The Patriarchal Culture of the School and The Problem of Change

When the detracking study began, several teachers and administrators told us that a small faction of male teachers known as the 'Good Old Boys', most of whom were athletic coaches, had long held power at Central. The hegemony of the Good Old Boys relied partly upon the ineffectiveness or unwillingness of past administrators to change the relations of power. As the principal, Bob Foster, stated, 'because of the [past] lack of leadership [at Central], [power in the school] came down to who could shout the loudest and that was the athletic department'. The Good Old Boys derived power from their status as coaches in a community that strongly supported the school's athletic teams, especially its football team. Given the school's history of weak leadership, poor academic standards, and support for athletics, it was not surprising that coaches at Central held and exercised power.

Over the years, little effort had been made to change the culture of the school, and many teachers doubted that anyone or anything could shake loose the Good Old Boys' hegemony of Central's school culture. Central's patriarchal culture, held firmly in place by the Good Old Boys, not only constrained the professional lives of women teachers, it also led to an environment of low academic expectations and stagnation for the students. In other words, the patriarchal school culture at Central High School reinforced the power relations around race and class that perpetuated tracking, as both the patriarchy and tracking relied upon the oppression of subordinate groups. (More about this in Chapter 4).

Encouraging Teacher Agency: Planting the Seeds for Reform

When the principal, Bob Foster, first came to the school in 1991, he noticed that 'the majority of the teaching staff did not believe that they could make a difference in their own lives or in the lives of the kids'. Therefore, one of his primary goals was to create a sense of empowerment and to build teacher leaders among the faculty. He immediately found this to be a very difficult task. Most teachers were initially very reluctant to work among themselves to make changes, as they were used to having the administration either impose change upon them or leave them to continue business as usual.

Mr Foster believed that if teachers were to take control over their lives, they would eventually make significant improvements in teaching and learning. More importantly, Bob Foster saw himself as a facilitator of teacher agency in the move to restructure. He stated: 'I simply try to implement and facilitate and let [the teachers] make decisions'. Bob Foster also had a personal commitment to detracking; when he arrived at the school, he reduced the number of separate tracks of algebra from five to two.

Betty Allen, an assistant principal at Central High School, also encouraged teachers to take ownership of the changes at the school. However, unlike Bob Foster, instead of making her role separate from that of the teachers in pushing reform, she allied herself with them and hoped that the staff would view her as a 'teacher who just isn't in the classroom anymore'. By being one of them, she hoped to facilitate the agency of reform-minded teachers by being a role model. After conducting research on the extent of tracking at Central, Ms Allen herself took charge in removing some of the basic level classes at Central in 1990. Still, the school remained highly tracked and, despite some interest among a number of teachers, there was not teacher consensus to alter the status quo.

Like Mr Foster and Ms Allen, the assistant superintendent, Frank Marsh, also believed that change at Central had to come from the teachers:

> I'm really convinced that this change in education has to come from the teachers, and our role then is to remove the hurdles and barriers and facilitate processes and cheerlead and compliment, go forward, and then it will happen. You can't mandate it.

The above statements by Central administrators suggest that they subscribed to the widely held belief among policy-makers and researchers that successful change is likely to evolve from a grass-roots effort arising from teachers. (This belief is reminiscent of the policy assumptions about teacher agency reviewed in Chapter 1.) Central's administrators argued that teachers must develop the ideas for reform themselves in order to create ownership of the change, and, in turn, that the role of the administration was to facilitate their efforts.

Restructuring Begins at Central High School

The seeds of reform at Central High School were finally planted when a national teachers' union leader gave a motivational speech at a staff development workshop for district teachers. After hearing his speech, a small group of approximately eight teachers, the majority of whom were women, brainstormed about possible changes that they could make at their school. After much deliberation, the teachers drew up plans for a pilot 'school-within-a-school' program: Central Lifetime Achievers or 'CLA'. The underlying goal of CLA was to improve the achievement of non-college prep track students, in particular minority students, by offering them a challenging program of study that would allow them to meet college entrance requirements. The CLA teachers created an inter-disciplinary, integrated curriculum across the core academic subjects in which teachers would follow students through their four years of high school. In the Fall of 1990, the first class of 125 formerly standard track students began the program. In the two years that followed, more students and teachers were added. The first graduating class of CLA students was very successful, raising standardized test scores and the school's college enrollment rate from 10 to 20 per cent; in one particular year, half of the graduating seniors enrolling in four-year colleges were CLA students.

In the Spring of 1992, buoyed by the success of the CLA program, several CLA teachers approached the administration about the possibility of implementing something similar to CLA on a school-wide level. These teachers had become aware of a request for proposals for school restructuring issued by the state department of education. The Central administration embraced the idea of school-wide restructuring and made the strategic decision to engage a broadbased group of support. They made an open invitation to the entire staff and community to meet to establish their ideal vision of a Central High School graduate and to generate ideas on how Central could be restructured to achieve that goal.

Over fifty people, including educators, parents, and community members, met at the school on a Saturday in the Spring of 1992 to develop a vision for Central High School. From the original group who met that day, a core group of sixteen people emerged, turning the vision into a plan for restructuring. This group of mostly women teachers called themselves the 'Idea Team'. The Idea Team had assistance throughout the process from a restructuring coach, a private consultant named Joan Dawson, who had significant experience working with schools. She was hired by Central's administration to assist in the development of the restructuring plan and later to help facilitate the implementation of the grant by serving as a neutral, outside party.

The Idea Team's proposal for restructuring included the plan to detrack the school by 'offering all students access to and assistance in a rich and challenging curriculum'. Based on their success with the CLA program, the Idea Team proposed that the school be divided into five 'houses' of 450 heterogeneously grouped students and teams of teachers who would remain attached to each house for four years. Each house would have its own administrator, counselor, and support staff. The purpose of the house model was to nurture a feeling of connection and a sense of family for the students. This would be enhanced through a homeroom period where faculty assist students in establishing personal, academic, and career goals. The Idea Team recognized the lack of academic and social guidance, both at home and at school, to be a major barrier to the success of many Central students.

The plan for detracking the school existed within a broader plan to revamp Central's curriculum. Under the proposed restructured curriculum, in the first two years of high school, all students would take a common set of interdisciplinary core courses taught by a team of four teachers in heterogeneous classes. In the upper grades, students would blend academic courses with a project-based course of study linked to the students' individual career goals. Community service and business internships would exist within the context of a college preparatory curriculum. This curriculum would be driven by an evaluation process centered on student products.

Support mechanisms, including learning centers, individualized programs, and study skills classes, would be provided so that students who had not formerly been academically successful could excel in detracked classes. To address students' other needs, the Idea Team also hoped to start both a health and social services center and a vocational resource center at the school.

Recognizing that teachers would have to learn new tools to teach heterogeneous groups, the proposal included a plan for partnering with a local university's school of education and instituting a peer-coaching professional development model. Teacher and student training in the use of state-of-the-art computer technology would be provided. Correspondingly, the restructuring proposal included a plan to use technology to enhance the management information system at the school in order to make record-keeping much more efficient for teachers.

One of the most interesting features of the restructuring proposal was the plan to change the school's calendar. The Idea Team proposed a 'custom calendar', which called for alternating a nine week quarter with a three week intercession. The custom calendar was proposed, in part, to raise the achievement of the school's large population of migrant students who had a high dropout rate. The new calendar would allow students to earn credits in shorter periods of time. Moreover, students seeking to remediate their skills or speed ahead could take courses during the intercession.

Central High School's elaborate and comprehensive restructuring proposal included statements of support from the district office, the school board, the local university, and the local teachers' union. In the Fall of 1992, the state granted Central $1.3 million of funding over five years under a law which provided funds for comprehensive school restructuring efforts. Central was selected among a small group of schools to receive this competitive grant from many schools state-wide, including another high school in their district.

In the end, the plans for school-wide change at Central High School were never instituted. Although reformers initially had a large amount of financial resources at their disposal, restructuring never occurred. One of the major factors in the downfall of reform at Central was in-fighting among the staff, which was executed on the battleground of gender politics. Due to the fierce political battles, the state removed the restructuring money after the end of the second year of reform efforts.

The following two chapters of this book are devoted to the chilling story of failed reform at Central due to gender politics between teachers at the school.

Notes

1   The three-year study was funded by a grant from the Lilly Endowment. Any opinions do not necessarily represent the positions or policies of the funder.
2   The research associates on this study were myself, Robert Cooper, Diane Hirshberg, Martin Lipton, Karen Ray, Irene Serna, Estella Williams, and Susan Yonezawa.
3   The final visit to the school was supported by a grant from the Office of Educational Research and Improvement, U.S. Department of Education (OERI-R-117-R900002). Any opinions do not necessarily represent the positions or policies of the funder.
4   This is not to say, however, that teachers are not part of a larger school and societal structure that reinforces tracking, or that other people in schools are not also active agents in creating and sustaining tracking. However, research has shown that many teachers favor tracking because they believe it substantially reduces their teaching duties, arguing that homogeneous grouping allows them to tailor instruction to students' needs (Oakes, 1985).

Today, many teachers still believe that tracking is a useful way to deal with the diversity of students in their classes (Carnegie Foundation for the Advancement of Teaching, 1988).

5   In her study of teachers and tracking, Finley (1984) found that the social status of a teacher rises and falls with the type of courses and students taught. Most secondary schools track teachers as well as students, although some schools rotate the teaching of low and high ability classes. The more qualified and more experienced teachers are generally found in the high tracks, and the opportunity to teach advanced classes is part of the reward system used by principals. This means that teachers in the lower tracks usually have less experience and are not as well qualified. Low track students are frequently taught math and science by teachers who are not certified to teach those subjects (Oakes, 1990).

6   During our study, the school was located in this facility. However, when I returned to the school in June, 1996, the school had relocated to a new facility away from the center of town. I was surprised to find that while most were happy to be at a new site, the move brought with it a host of new administrative dilemmas, and thus was not seen as entirely positive by the teachers. Additionally, the architectural structure of the new campus grouped teachers into separate, subject-centered buildings.

3   Teachers at Central High School: Identities and Ideologies

This chapter introduces the reader to the factions of teachers at Central High School. The teachers at Central fell into three distinct groups. First, the 'Idea Team', a faction made up mostly of female teachers, fought against the prevailing structure and culture at Central in their struggle to bring about detracking. The Idea Team created the plan for restructuring at Central High. Second, the 'Good Old Boys', a faction of entrenched male teachers, defended the status quo in the school, including tracking, and the dominant ideology that held it in place. Third, the 'Middle Group', a large group of teachers, who, unlike the Idea Team and the Good Old Boys, did not constitute a definable faction in political terms and whose actions did not as profoundly influence the course of reform.[1]

This chapter focuses on each group's identity and ideology. In the identity section, each group and its constituent members are described in terms of their individual characteristics (e.g., departmental affiliation and years of experience) and how they were defined as a group (e.g., their monikers and the roles they played in the school). The bulk of this chapter is devoted to a discussion of teachers' ideologies in each of the factions, given the importance of ideology in micropolitical analysis and its salience in explaining the role of teachers in reform. As the literature reviewed in Chapter 1 suggests, an examination of teachers' ideological subcultures helps explain the ideological differences behind the struggle for power between the Idea Team and the Good Old Boys and why ideological hegemony persisted at Central High School. Ideological subcultures also provide important insight into teacher agency in reform and its intersection with the larger societal structure and culture.

In fact, the two political factions at Central constituted extremely strong ideological subcultures. In this chapter, I analyze the common ideologies of the Idea Team and the Good Old Boys concerning several important areas relating to their roles in reform: 1) the role of the teacher; 2) constructions of student ability; 3) explanations for low student achievement; and 4) perspectives on detracking and the complexity of reform. There are stark differences between the Idea Team and the Good Old Boys in each of these areas. Since the Idea Team and the Good Old Boys had contrasting representations of how 'school' ought to be defined, of how their roles as a teachers ought to be defined, and of what they expected of students, they had different roles in reform. On the other hand, the Middle Group did not constitute an ideological subculture of like-minded teachers, unlike the Idea Team and the Good Old Boys, except that the Middle Group shared an unwillingness to become political players in reform and tended to be more isolated as teachers.

In sum, this chapter answers the questions of what ideological ties bind each group of teachers together, what 'school' means to them, and what reform means to them. In discussing the ideologies of each group, I attempt to make a distinction between statements that reflect teachers' ideologies and statements that reflect teachers' efforts to establish order to their practices (Shilling, 1992). By understanding the ideologies of the various groups, we can begin to unravel the gender politics of the reform process at Central, which is discussed in Chapter 4. I now begin with a comparison of the identities and ideologies of the Idea Team and the Good Old Boys. I discuss the Middle Group separately at the end of this chapter.

Who are the Idea Team and the Good Old Boys?

The Idea Team

The Idea Team evolved from the group of fifty people who met at Central to develop the initial vision for restructuring. From this larger group of fifty, dubbed the 'critical mass group', sixteen teachers represented the core group interested in pushing the reform forward. As the principal, Bob Foster, explained:

> [I]f we could have a critical mass of change agents on the staff, then the people pursuing the change would not be subjected to the same type of negative pressure that the CLA group had been. . . . [O]ut of that critical mass group, we basically self-selected 16 people who we called the 'Idea Team'.

In fact, according to assistant principal, Betty Allen, the name 'The Idea Team' accurately stated the job of these teachers during the proposal development process: 'This was where ideas got generated, sorted through, and carved out'. Four members of the Idea Team (all white women) wrote the restructuring proposal, and these women, including the assistant principal, were the people who were most associated with the restructuring grant from that point onward.

In total, the Idea Team comprised sixteen people, the majority of whom were teachers in a variety of departments, including math, English, science, social studies, bilingual education, and vocational education. The most active members and the majority (N=9) of the Idea Team were white women in their late forties. Most of them had been teaching for over twenty years. Of the nine white women, three taught college-preparatory-track classes, three taught a mixture of regular and college-preparatory classes, one taught vocational education, one was an assistant principal, and one was a parent of a student at Central. A tenth woman on the Idea Team was a young Latina (fewer than five years experience) who taught English as a Second Language (ESL). The eleventh woman on the Idea Team was an African-American parent of a student at Central.

Of the five male teachers on the Idea Team, four were white males who had taught for ten or more years. One taught honors classes, one vocational education, and two taught a combination of college-prep and regular track classes in a variety of subject — areas. There was also one Latino male teacher who taught English as a Second Language (ESL) and had been teaching for fewer than five years.

Although membership in the group was voluntary and open, this was not a fluid group: one teacher (female, African-American, over twenty years teaching experience) did join after the original group was formed; and, one of the original members (white, female, over twenty years teaching) subsequently left the school to take a curriculum development position. Neither of the two parents remained active in restructuring after the initial idea generating sessions.

Overall, the Idea Team was described by the school's restructuring coach as 'a group very interested in kids and changing things to make them work for kids and being innovative and taking risks. Those people are normally very polite, very nice and frankly female'. In addition to being referred to as the Idea Team or the Facilitating Team (later in the restructuring process), this group had several other more derogatory names, including the 'Dream Team', or simply the 'Dreamers', which the Good Old Boys used to refer to them. As school board member Bill Bathgate described the Idea Team: 'They are the dreamers. They are the ones who dream up the good things that should come along'. He noted that every school has a group of dreamers, and accordingly, a group resistant to change, like the Good Old Boys.

The Good Old Boys

Unlike the Idea Team whose origins sprang from the restructuring efforts at Central, the Good Old Boys existed as a faction in the school long before restructuring began. As mentioned, the Good Old Boys had for years covertly ruled the school through bully tactics and had maintained the status quo of a traditional high school structure, including tracking. Before profiling the characteristics of the Good Old Boys, it should be noted that the sobriquet was widely used among faculty and administration at the school, including the Good Old Boys themselves. All of the Good Old Boys proudly and forthrightly identified themselves as part of this group in their interviews with us. They were also referred to by other teachers as the 'Naysayers'. When I asked several of the Good Old Boys where the 'Good Old Boys' nickname came from, answers ranged from 'it just sort of appeared one day' to 'it was put on us'.

The Good Old Boys were not insulted by their widely used nickname. When I asked one of the Good Old Boys if they objected to the moniker, he answered: 'The hell with it. I've been called [worse names], so what's the difference. I am what I am'. Some, however, felt a little more ambivalent about the term as representing an accurate picture of their beliefs. As one teacher explained, 'Being a child of the sixties, it's kind of an unusual situation to find yourself in, to be called a Good Old Boy. But I guess if the shoe fits . . .'

For me, the identification of this faction known as the Good Old Boys came immediately when I began data collection at the school in Fall of 1992. The principal first introduced this faction by simply describing a group of people who were 'very vocal and very antagonistic toward everyone else. Most of these teachers have a tendency to be very angry people who don't deal with conflict well'. He did not refer to them as the Good Old Boys. Similarly, the assistant superintendent also did not refer to the Good Old Boys moniker when he described a group of 'real strong people who have the attitude "I'll be here when you're not"'. Later in our data collection, another educator at Central described the Good Old Boys as 'male, very veteran, very able to be very outspoken, and not at all unwilling to be abrasive to the point of abusive in order to get their way, in order not to have to change'.

This view of the Good Old Boys was echoed by the assistant principal Betty Allen, who explained that traditionally at Central these were the teachers 'who could and would stand up in the faculty meetings and begin a loud, angry discourse or those who came and ranted and raved in the main office . . . and got control'. In addition, Betty

Allen suggested that the Good Old Boys not only had political clout on campus, but also frequently called school board members and district administrators to voice their strong opinions. This long-time political strategy of engendering district level support evoked strong resentment from other staff members. As one teacher explained:

> Individuals here on this staff [the Good Old Boys] have a history of running to the board and running to certain individuals in the district office and complaining about things like the squeaky wheel . . . And that's been tolerated. Whereas the rest of us will generally try follow normal procedures.

In general, there was some interesting debate at Central about the size of the faction known as the Good Old Boys. Depending on whom one spoke with, the size of the faction ranged from three to thirteen! A male teacher (not a Good Old Boy) described them as 'a small group, sort of like a rat pack that runs around and likes to pick on people'. This teacher estimated the number at ten. Another male teacher thought they were a 'group of . . . seven or eight: Three ring leaders and a couple of *yes, sirs* who follow along with whatever the other guys say'. Interestingly, a woman teacher on the Idea Team thought the Good Old Boys comprised thirteen members and in fact called themselves the 'Dirty 13'.

Strictly speaking, I identified a core group of nine Good Old Boys who fit the profile of being in their late forties, having been at the school for over twenty years, and who were described as 'entrenched staff' with strong union ties. These nine Good Old Boys taught in a variety of different departments, including math, science, social studies, physical education, and foreign language. The majority (N=6) taught honors and/college preparatory track classes. In addition, of great importance, most of the Good Old Boys either coached sports or had been coaches at one time in their career. The racial breakdown was six whites, two Asian-Americans, and one Latino.

One explanation for the range in estimates of the number of Good Old Boys involved younger teachers who had reportedly been socialized into the Good Boys faction because they shared a common bond with the Good Old Boys: they coached sports and/or fitted into what one Good Old Boy referred to as the 'traditional jock' stereotype. This notion of recruiting or socializing newer members was of concern to the Idea Team members. As one Idea Team teacher stated: 'They recruit young males so that they can perpetuate themselves'.

One of the Good Old Boys, science teacher and football coach Marty Wong, explained the importance of the socialization process for both the Good Old Boys and their younger 'recruits':

> Central used to be a school where you came here as a teacher at age 25 or so and you would live out . . . your last years here . . . The old administrators and the old coaching staff, they're the same guys who were here when I was going to high school. And when you come in, you jump right in with the boys and they teach you the tricks of the trade . . . To be able to survive, you've got to get the tricks of the trade. Like I said, there have been six principals since I've been here.

This teacher was very evasive, however, when I asked him to describe the 'tricks of the trade'. He jokingly answered, jingling his keys, 'you've got to get a lot of keys'. I think he meant that only those with a connection to the 'Boys' were privileged enough to get the keys to the 'house', in this case, Central. This teacher had been at the school for over twenty years and he proudly stated: 'Are you familiar with the TV series "Welcome Back Kotter?" That's me. I grew up here, the whole bit. I coach football, I've been activities director, and department chair. I've done all that'.

Another notable feature of the Good Old Boys was their poor relations with and even animosity from the current school administration, due in part to their boisterous behavior. As math teacher Ralph Boskey stated in an interview: 'I am very surprised you're talking to me because I am not real popular with some of the administrators because I shoot my mouth off when I am mad'. For example, if he were required to teach a new type of math course, he answered, 'I'd scream and holler and make everybody know exactly what my feelings are on it'.

Just as the identities of the Good Old Boys and the Idea Team were strikingly different, so too were their ideologies about education. I now proceed to comparing them along several dimensions, beginning with a discussion of how each group conceived of their role as teachers.

What are the Ideologies that Bind Each Group Together?

Conceptions of Their Role as Teachers: 'We Can Change the World' vs. 'That's Not My Job'

The Idea Team

By deliberately changing the nature of teachers' roles through new organizational structures, the proposed restructuring plan called into question teachers' beliefs about how their role as teachers ought to be defined. The teachers in the Idea Team and the Good Old Boys conceived of their lives as teachers very differently. The Idea Team, grounded in the notion of 'we can change the world', emphasized altruism as the reason they initially pursued a career in teaching and as their continuing motivation. Barbara Cooper, a math teacher, explained this altruistic tendency:

> [S]omebody has to sacrifice something for the better of others . . . Most teachers are pretty philanthropic. We [teachers] did not come into this because we wanted to be wealthy. We came into this because we thought being a teacher would help kids . . . When it comes to a kid and his future, we can't afford not to try [something new].

Similarly, many of the Idea Team teachers discussed the substantial amount of time they invested in Central High School. A math teacher explained: 'School is everything. I come at 7.30, invariably I'm here until 4.30 or 5.00, then I take work home with me. . . . I have a family of my own [but] from September till June I'm just like school, school, school, school'.

Idea Team members also viewed their job as teachers and their involvement with restructuring at Central as integral and important parts of their lives. The Idea Team treated the extra time and energy involved in reform efforts as not only altruistic for students but also in their own self-interest. Keith Evans, a science teacher, explained this:

> It's where we work. It's our profession. Why do I do it? I wonder myself sometimes. My students asked me: 'why are you going to the board meeting, do you get paid?' I said no. . . . In other words, you can sit around and complain about [the status quo] and that's sort of negative, or you can get in and do something.

As Mr Evans went on to add, for him, altruism for students and his self-interest as a teacher nicely dove-tailed: 'I like the administration . . . [but] that's not why I come to work everyday. It's the students. And if I'm doing worse by them that hurts me'.

For the Idea Team, the role of the teacher included being emancipators of students disadvantaged by traditional school practices and the dominant ideology of a false meritocracy that supports such practices. This statement by Lucy Berg, an English teacher on the Idea Team, illustrates this belief:

> My biggest hope is [to] find a way for all teachers to think that all kids can learn. To acknowledge and honor that would be hopeful . . . I just

try to have faith that good will win. I'm sorry I think it's good and evil.
I do. I think it's evil to keep people down when especially those
people are children.

Through their discussions of reform, the Idea Team hoped to convince
the rest of the faculty that tracking perpetuates misconceptions that
minority and low income students are less capable of academic achievement than their white, middle income counterparts. Lucy Berg's talk of
reforming schools so that students are 'not kept down', is reminiscent
of Giroux and McLaren's (1986) conception of schools as sites of social
transformation or Kanpol's (1992) notion of 'cultural political resistance'
in which teachers use critical pedagogy to raise awareness about how the
organization of schooling perpetuates the inherent inequities in society.

Although only isolated examples of critical pedagogy were taking
place in classrooms at Central High School, some of the Idea Team
teachers discussed it in connection with their plans to make schools
more democratic. For example, John Perez, a member of the Idea Team
who created a program for recently immigrated students with no prior
experience with schooling, discussed his interest in critical pedagogy:
'Teachers cannot be facilitators of critical pedagogy until they empower
themselves. So I don't feel like I'm empowered enough to do that yet.
I don't have enough *ganas* to do that yet. But it's going to happen. Just
you wait'. For some Idea Team teachers, the goal was to empower low
income and minority students by enlightening them to the system which
continued to disadvantage them. The overall goal, as Mr Perez suggested,
was that students could eventually 'change their own situation'. As you
will soon see, such notions as critical pedagogy, altruism, and a holistic
commitment to school (the intertwining of their personal and professional lives) could not have been more antithetical to how the Good
Old Boys viewed their role as teachers.

The Good Old Boys

In contrast to the Idea Team, the Good Old Boys viewed teaching as
an 'eight-to-three' job whose sole occupational purpose was to teach
subject matter to students. For example, unlike the more holistic approach of the Idea Team teachers, math teacher and union president
Bill Dalton viewed his personal life as completely separate from his
professional life: 'I've decided it's better to live away from where you
teach. When I first started teaching in the midwest I had the top of my
convertible slit two times . . . It's a good idea not to live too close to
your school. You make enemies no matter what you do'.

Moreover, the Good Old Boys simply were not comfortable dealing with the affective, emotional side of students, preferring to restrict
their focus to academics. In fact, one basis for the Good Old Boys'
resistance to restructuring at Central was the 'touchy-feely' nature of
the reforms. For example, a social studies teacher who was against the
house and team teaching models of organization criticized these reforms
on such grounds: 'Frankly I don't really care what other teachers think
about kids because I don't want that to cloud my judgment . . . I want
to worry about what's going on in here, and not that they're screwing
up in somebody else's class or that they're going to screw up in my
class'.

Similarly, another Good Old Boy stated: 'I understand that kids
come to us with some problems and . . . we need to be compassionate
. . . [However], we have so many groups and organizations on campus
[for] these kids'. He was referring to the special programs at Central
which had been established for disadvantaged students, such as programs for teen mothers and for students with alcohol and drug abuse
problems. These were issues he did not feel he had to deal with in the
context of his classroom.

When asked what his ideal teaching assignment might be, a social
studies teacher answered:

> I would like to have seven or eight kids who are highly motivated so
> that we can go out on the lawn and talk about things. . . . The kids
> could ask questions and we can talk about things, talk about import-
> ant things. That would be my ideal. Almost like if you think back to
> Ancient Greece, with Socrates talking to his pupils.

Science teacher Norm Shiro reiterated that he prefers teaching students who are 'highly motivated, pay attention, and are not discipline
problems'.

In general, the Good Old Boys believed that the role of a teacher
was simply to cope with, but not improve a student's individual situation. As one teacher stated, 'How do you inspire all kids to have that
drive? Beats me. I think some kids are just born with it. . . . If they've
got family support, that helps too'. Another teacher succinctly summed
it up: 'If you don't have enthusiasm, I can't give you what's important in your life'. The Good Old Boys did not see themselves as trans-
formers of schools or as people who could make a difference in the
lives of students from disadvantaged backgrounds or those who needed
more guidance and advice. The Good Old Boys accepted, rather than
deconstructed, the widely held societal belief that highly motivated

students are those who are most deserving of a good education. The Good Old Boys were most comfortable when the limits of their job as a teacher were bounded and traditional. They preferred to be removed from the social milieu and problems of their students. Thus, as will be seen in Chapter 4, they fought the Idea Team's restructuring efforts (e.g., detracking and house model of organization), believing that they were disruptive to their professional lives at Central.

Constructions of Student Ability: 'All Kids have a Gift' vs. 'You Can't Mix Apples and Oranges'

The Idea Team

With detracking as a major component of the restructuring effort at Central, teachers' constructions of student ability, which are always important, took on an even more magnified role. In terms of ideology, the Idea Team and the Good Old Boys could not have been more dia-metrically opposed. The Idea Team fervently believed that all students had the ability to learn. Thus, the role of the teacher was to provide opportunities in the classroom for all students to excel. The Idea Team teachers also viewed Central's track structure as having perpetuated the belief that white students, who were over-represented in the college preparatory classes, were innately intelligent, and minority students, who comprised the lower track classes, were not.

Idea Team teachers had different reasons for viewing student ability this way. One Idea Team teacher viewed the construction of student ability in its most rudimentary form: 'Why are we assuming that the kids who can barely get out an English sentence . . . are automatically incapable . . . [of] the idea of going to college?' Another Idea Team teacher based his conception that all students could learn on actual past experiences: 'The CLA program has done amazing things for [standard track] kids. Because all of a sudden somebody says "you can do this"'.

Idea Team teachers strongly believed in the social construction of ability (Berger and Luckmann, 1967; Oakes et al., 1997). For example, a science teacher believed that while some students had 'special talent or God-given talent. . . . A lot of those kids are [in upper track classes] because their parents want them to be'. By suggesting that while there are 'traditionally academically gifted' students, 'there are all kinds of gifts' that students have which the current school structure and culture does not acknowledge, this teacher echoed the belief held by other Idea Team teachers that all students can learn.

Similarly, another teacher talked about the fact that while she believes that 'all kids have a gift', there are some teachers who 'say there are the *haves* and the *have-nots*'. Discussing her own daughter who is very artistic, but has not succeeded academically, she stated: 'I don't put her in the *have-not* category. I put her in the category of students who have not yet achieved some things that other kids at age 13 have'. Several Idea Team teachers stated their belief in multiple types of intelligence and that their role as a teacher was to give students the chance to excel in various ways based on the children's individual strengths (Gardner, 1983).

In their effort to disprove the myths about innate student intelligence (and the overlap with race) that legitimated the track structure at Central, the Idea Team teachers made special efforts with students who might not otherwise have been provided with opportunities to shine. As an Idea Team teacher explained:

> I have a little girl in my class who is fifteen years old who just had a baby. I asked her, 'why don't you do your homework?'. And she said, 'Mrs Alvarez, when I go home, I have to take care of my baby'. . . . So for kids like that you have to understand. You have to try to do as much as you can for them. [You say], 'come in at lunch time, I'll work with you'. Or give them an extra day to do it if you have to.

The Idea Team teachers were particularly concerned that many Central students, by virtue of their life circumstances, were viewed *prima facie* as 'not smart'. They sought to convince their colleagues that just because a student 'lives in the barrio' does not mean that a student is not gifted. Rather, such disadvantaged students might need different opportunities to achieve (such as interdisciplinary projects rather than textbook assignments) or might require special efforts or compassion by the teacher (such as arranging to meet students for extra tutoring outside of class time). In the end, Idea Team teachers connected their role as teachers with their belief in the socially constructed nature of student ability by attempting to bring out the best in all students.

The Good Old Boys

In contrast to the Idea Team, the Good Old Boys viewed ability as fixed: high intelligence, an innate quality, existing only in some students, not in all students. Veteran science teacher Walter Brown explained his perspective, which many of the Good Old Boys shared: '[It] may just be simple intellectual ability. Some kids are just born with it. I don't know if I want to get into this controversial thing. Some kids have got it and some kids don't'. Another Good Old Boy stated: 'On the freeway you have speed limits and you have minimum speed limits. If the person can't reach 45, they shouldn't be able to go on that freeway'. These statements reveal that the Good Old Boys subscribed to conventional beliefs about intelligence, which are deeply embedded in Western culture and which serve to hold tracking in place. According to Cohen, Kemper, and Swanson (1995), a belief system that credits only one type of intelligence will obstruct educational reform.

Unlike the Idea Team teachers who passionately believed that all students, regardless of race, social class, or gender, were capable of learning, the comments by the Good Old Boys suggested that these variables entered into the Good Old Boys construction of student ability. For example, a veteran math teacher felt 'gang-type kids' (who are primarily Latino), currently placed in the standard track, could not work well with (white) college preparatory track students in group situations. He explained:

> I think a lot of these college prep kids are getting smart enough that they have their own study groups. I don't know ... when you start putting standard kids in, a lot of those kids have completely different habits, or they've got different cultures, different lifestyles, and these other kids [college prep] have been together. It's really difficult to break them in. It makes it real tough on [the college preparatory track students].

Another teacher felt similarly about the low innate ability of students in the standard track: 'I think that you can push them to their maximum ... but just giving them a college prep curriculum is pushing most of them way beyond what they can handle'. He felt that the students currently placed in standard tracks were simply incapable of learning more complicated material. Another Good Old Boy reiterated, 'you can lead a horse to water but you can't make him drink. . . . You can have high expectations for the kids, but you have to be realistic about it'.

However, when asked about whether they saw any difference in the student composition of high versus low track classes in terms of race or ethnicity, several of the Good Old Boys told us that they did not see any differences or that they simply did not pay attention to such issues. In this regard, they took a 'color-blind perspective'. For example, as a social studies teacher stated: 'I don't look at kids as minority or whatever. They're just kids'. This was rather naive, given that the tracks at Central were so racially identifiable, with Latino students concentrated in the low tracks and white students concentrated in the college preparatory tracks. Of course, the Idea Team completely disagreed with this view, and, a main purpose of their restructuring efforts was to bring attention to and eliminate the racially inequitable school sorting system.

There was also evidence of a gender bias in the Good Old Boys' constructions of student ability. Math teacher Ralph Boskey explained that males and females have different learning styles, particularly in math: 'When you work in small group environments, the females, even if they're part of the male group, as long as they're not the only female in the group, will learn better. . . . There is less stress for them in that group environment than when they're sitting at their desk. Males seem to learn better sitting at their desk'. He added that because of this gender difference in learning styles, he occasionally allows students to work in groups. He said he lets the 'girls who have a buddy in the class' work together. He stated that the boys sometimes join the group 'so they can learn something and get a date at the same time'. Clearly, the Idea Team teachers who were primarily female and held progressive feminist viewpoints likely viewed this ideology as insulting and damaging to the education of young women at Central.

In truth, the Good Old Boys were at least cognizant of these gender issues in their conceptions of student ability. They seemed to feel as though their views on 'learning styles' were progressive and sensitive to students' needs. For example, in attempting to fix the problem that 'males dominate' in his classes, social studies teacher Peter Owen explained: 'I've been called on it and I try to correct it . . . I put quotes on the board everyday and we discuss them. And when we start off, there's always certain males that want to dominate conversations, especially in my college prep and honors classes'. Although he was trying to counteract this gender effect by calling on students at random, Mr Owen was not willing to 'shut down' the males who were eager to participate in his class. In fact, Mr Owen appeared to be contributing to the problem through his stereotypical view of gender differences in learning style.

In summary, as one Good Old Boy emphatically stated, 'different kids need different techniques in order to learn up to their potential. And it's unrealistic to think otherwise'. These traditional constructions of student ability helped the Good Old Boys explain the problem of low achievement that existed for minority students at Central, allowing them to justify the status quo. As will be discussed in the next section, the Idea Team's desire to dismantle the status quo was in fact based in their belief that by changing school structures, teachers might be led to think differently about student ability.

> *Explanations for Low Student Achievement: 'Everything Around has Changed, Except the Schools' vs. 'It's the Family Structure that's Causing the Schools to Fail'*

Idea Team

According to the Idea Team teachers, Central High was not educating a large portion of its population. In keeping with their ideologies about student ability, the Idea Team viewed this problem as emanating from ineffective organizational arrangements and an outdated, uninspiring curriculum, and not rooted in the students themselves. The problem of low student achievement, particularly among ethnic and linguistic minority students, came from the intractability of the traditional secondary school structure and the ideologies about student ability which it reinforced. In illustrating this viewpoint, one Idea Team teacher stated: 'I would like to change a lot of things, and my argument tends to be that in the last few years everything around us has changed, except the schools. That can't be right!'. On the issue of tracking this teacher took a rather elemental stance: 'Do we keep it that way just because its been that way forever?'.

Math teacher Christy Johnson strongly believed that, 'if there are kids who are damaged, which is most of my [general track] students, then it is because the elementary school convinced them that they were stupid'. Of note, Ms Johnson felt that high achieving students would not only not be harmed by detracking, but that in fact they 'would benefit tremendously by being with other kids who have to struggle to get answers'. In general, Idea Team teachers recognized the entrenchment of tracking and the structure and culture that reinforces it.

Recognizing the impact of teacher ideology on student performance, several Idea Team teachers squarely placed the burden of low student achievement on teachers who felt some students incapable of learning. According to the Idea Team teachers, a core problem in education was 'teachers oppressing students' or 'teachers who chose the wrong profession' or 'teachers who are not life long learners'. Of course, the Idea Team did not consider themselves as part of this group of teachers, but rather implicitly placed the blame on the Good Old Boys.

The Idea Team teachers genuinely believed that by changing teachers' beliefs and the accompanying traditional school structure at Central, they could raise student achievement. As one teacher argued: 'If we don't expect that kids have their doors open, then they won't have their doors open. It's real simple'. Similarly, another teacher, keying on the need to change classroom practices, stated: 'Rows and aisles, read the text, answer the questions at the end of the book. It doesn't make it [work], you know'.

These teachers acknowledged that the benefits of detracking could best be realized in a racially mixed setting because only in such a setting could they prove the social construction of ability as it relates to race. An Idea Team teacher stated that Central had the 'perfect student population' to do something dramatic, like detracking, because 'it is not all white. . . . It's the real world'. By changing the structure of the school, the teachers felt they could prove that formerly low achieving minority students could indeed join the ranks of their white peers in the college preparatory track.

The Idea Team sought fundamental school restructuring because they believed that the existing distribution of resources in their school only advantaged those in high track classes and that a redistribution would actually work in improving the achievement of disadvantaged students (Oakes, Gamoran and Page, 1992). That a number of the Idea Team teachers had positive experiences in raising student achievement through the CLA program led them to be optimistic about the possibilities of changes on a larger scale. Thus, the Idea Team sought to fundamentally transform what 'school' means by moving toward an innovative structure which included detracking and a nurturing, supportive school culture in which teachers shared the belief that all students can learn.

The Good Old Boys

In direct contrast to the Idea Team, the Good Old Boys believed that schools were not the problem; rather, it was the students. While they shared the belief that in fact the school was not educating a large population of their students, they viewed this as a problem endemic to the 'type' of student that was now attending Central. This was duly noted in the Good Old Boys' conceptions of student ability discussed in the previous section.

According to the Good Old Boys, the problem of low student achievement was rooted in 'broken' families who did not value education. One of the Good Old Boys, a social studies teacher, illustrated this belief: 'I don't care what anybody tells you, it's the family structure that's causing the schools to fail. I can teach a kid and give him the material, but I can't make the kid learn'. Two other Good Old Boys agreed:

I'm not about to put twenty-two years of my life on the line because somebody thinks kids can learn together and they'll become more of a family unit and that schools should replace the home because the home society is so screwed up. So, schools should replace the home. I don't buy that. (Math teacher)

It's hard though because there's only so much you can do with the kids. We don't get really well-motivated, well-educated kids. Most come from not ideal family situations, they're not very well-motivated . . . and it's really hard to do anything in that situation, no matter what you do as teachers, there's just some kids, nothing is going to help them, and nothing is going to solve your problems. (Social Studies teacher)

As these comments suggest, the Good Old Boys rejected the notion that the problem of low student achievement lay within the structure of schools or the quality of teaching that was provided to students. Rather, they believed that there was little the school could do for students who came from 'not ideal' family situations. By blaming the breakdown of the family structure in American society for the problem of low student achievement, these teachers avoided blaming themselves.

> *Perspectives on Detracking: 'I Can See How Destructive Homogeneous Grouping is' vs. 'Detracking is the Worst Way To Go'*

The Idea Team

The Idea Team teachers saw tracking as a highly problematic school structure that was especially damaging to minority students who were disproportionately placed in the low tracks. For some teachers, this belief was rooted in their personal experience. English teacher Lucy Berg described the discussion among Idea Team teachers which led to detracking being incorporated in Central's restructuring proposal: 'I continued to say how I felt about students who were labeled and students who are not given access [to a challenging curriculum] and students who are trapped, who can't climb out of the ruts. Other people testified to that in terms of specific students they'd had, or specific experiences they themselves had gone through as students'.

For example, in the case of another English teacher, Terri Jamison, her personal experience of having her daughter placed into the low track influenced her views about detracking:

My daughter . . . was stuck at the low end, in the lowest math class in the school. She is a bright little girl, but she's a divergent thinker so she doesn't focus . . . I have a real thing about [tracking] because I have a bright little girl who would have been in the toilet. I can see how destructive homogeneous grouping is and that's why I don't like it because I saw it in action and I had to fight hard to keep my kid from believing what she was being taught in school, which was that she is incapable of doing math. And now this is the kid who wants to be an astrophysicist!

Not surprisingly, Ms Jamison was one of the spearheads in advocating heterogeneous grouping and the move to reform the English curriculum. As Fullan (1991) states, a teacher's personal experience often affects his/her ideologies about education. Ms Jamison not only saw how tracking ultimately limited students' future opportunities, but more importantly, she realized that tracking relied upon ideological hegemony: her daughter was 'taught to believe' she was incapable of doing math, thereby legitimizing her low track placement.

For some Idea Team teachers, their interest in dismantling tracking resulted from their independent research on the topic. For example, a teacher stated: 'As I understand it, I've read Jeannie Oakes' articles and other things, and if handled intelligently with an eye on reality, in a detracked environment the top kids will still be the top kids. In fact, they'll be *topper* than they were before because they'll have more opportunities to prove their *toppedness*'.

While all of the Idea Team teachers hoped to disrupt the status quo at Central High School by offering all students access to a rich and challenging curriculum, they differed in the degree of detracking that they felt was feasible. Certainly the four women writers of the proposal were the strongest proponents of full scale detracking (including the removal of honors classes). These teachers felt that detracking was likely to be successful school-wide, based on their positive experience in teaching a college preparatory curriculum to low achieving students in the CLA program. However, a science and math teacher, who described himself as a 'dissenting minority' on the Idea Team, accepted most but not all of the restructuring plan. Particularly on the issue of detracking, he felt that the Idea Team members who had been teachers in the CLA program were 'too idealistic'. He commented: 'I don't think they have enough experience with what they're suggesting. I teach everybody in this school, all levels, the lowest math class to the highest and everything in between and I'm saying, "do you think you can do this?"'. While his mission was to increase access through heterogeneous grouping, he questioned the feasibility of their comprehensive, full scale detracking plan.

The Good Old Boys

Concerning detracking, the Good Old Boys uniformly shared several strong reasons against it. First, they did not see tracking as problematic. In fact, tracking made sense to them and fit in with their conception of schooling: give the best resources to the top students; the rest need less. Stated differently, a social studies teacher argued: 'My philosophy is . . . that detracking is the furthest away from individualizing instruction that you can get. The more tracks you have, the closer you get to kids' individual abilities . . . then detracking is the worst way to go from that perspective'.

All of the Good Old Boys described their teaching techniques as 'traditional'. Therefore, much of their fear and dislike of detracking came from their misconceptions of the pedagogical methods for teaching heterogeneous groups as wholly unworkable. As one Good Old Boy stated: 'The idea of cooperative learning is the smart guy does it and we all copy it. It has been a disaster'. Another Good Old Boy, science teacher Marty Wong, also criticized cooperative learning, emphatically stating 'I'm into the basics. When I teach my Bio Lab class, we read aloud. We're still into the old structure'. Similarly, math teacher Ralph Boskey criticized their new math curriculum because it 'emphasize[d] group work, group product, and presentations'.

Not only did they view the methods that might be used in detracked classes as unworkable, but the very notion of teaching heterogeneous classes was antithetical to their sense of reality in the classroom. A teacher stated: 'I don't think it's practical to say that you're going to take standard kids and just give them a college prep curriculum'. Another Good Old Boy saw detracking as 'dumping all the kids in one pile and teaching to the middle'. Several of the Good Old Boys made more blatant comments about their lack of efficacy in teaching heterogeneous groups. Veteran math teacher and union president Bill Dalton discussed his views:

> You know it looks good on paper . . . The smart ones will teach the other ones so you don't have to do it. Well it doesn't work that way. It works pretty well if they're not too far apart, but there's some place there if the range gets too large, it doesn't work any more, or at least I can't make it work. Maybe somebody else can. I've always liked working with the basic kids . . . I've never taught algebra or any of the higher math . . . I've never been interested in teaching those classes . . . I'm too old to learn new tricks. I'll stay with what I've got.

Incidentally, Mr Dalton had been a plastics teacher at Central and when the program was phased out, he began to teach in the math department.

According to Bob Foster, Mr Dalton chose to teach basic track classes because they required less preparation time, and thus allowed him time for his union responsibilities.

A social studies teacher, Peter Owen, explained that he too could not make heterogeneous grouping work: 'I'm very opposed to it. I can see it in my geography classes. I try to hit the middle and then your upper end kids already did the work and they want more. And your special education kids haven't got their names on the paper yet . . . You have all these different ability levels and what do you do?'.

Some of the Good Old Boys' comments about their apparent inability to make detracking work were couched in terms of its inappropriateness in certain subjects. Science teacher Walter Brown explained:

> I don't know how Jaime Escalante did it. Except, I'll tell you one thing, math is different than science. Math does not require reading ability . . . You can maybe bring kids up in math if you give them a narrow set of things [to learn], but how do you move kids ahead in math and ahead in language [which is required for science] at the same time?

Although the Good Old Boys may have some legitimate arguments why some subjects are more difficult to detrack than others, the fact is, we heard that detracking was not possible in any subject, including such different disciplines as math, English, science, or social studies.

Several of the Good Old Boys suggested that they had already tried heterogeneous grouping and that it had not worked. One Good Old Boy after another told us: 'We tried it, and it was a miserable failure'. In actuality, these explanations had little if any plausibility, since detracking had not yet been tried in any wholesale way at the school, having only been piloted in CLA in which none of the Good Old Boys were involved. These statements indicate how fearful the Good Old Boys were of not only altering their sense of order, but also being challenged and possibly failing.

Moreover, since teaching high track classes did not necessarily correlate with high status for teachers at Central, both low track and high track Good Old Boys resisted reform based on their unwillingness to break their routines and perform extra work. As one teacher defiantly explained: 'I have the cream cake schedule of all the teachers in the department . . . I have three periods of algebra one honors and two periods of algebra two'.

In many ways, it seemed that the Good Old Boys dislike of detracking was grounded in simple self-interest. They did not want to expend the time and effort that teaching new courses, or new groups of students, would entail. As science teacher Norm Shiro explained, he hoped never to teach the newly proposed integrated science class because, in his own words, 'I've been teaching what I've been teaching for several years so I've pretty much got it refined where I've got all the activities arranged, and it goes along pretty smoothly'.

The Good Old Boys' unwillingness to do extra work at this stage of their careers is consistent with Sikes et al.'s (1985) study of teachers' life histories. In phase four (age forty to fifty), male teachers settle into their careers, as promotion after age forty becomes increasingly unlikely. Men teachers generally become complacent with their positions, having put more effort into their careers at an earlier age, and are less willing to invest extra time into teaching. For women teachers, on the other hand, phase four often represents a period of career growth, as they often are no longer involved with raising their own children. Not surprisingly, the above gender differences in career objectives for phase four directly correlates with the scenario at Central: The Idea Team, mostly women in their forties, were willing to put in the effort for reform, while the Good Old Boys, men in their forties, vehemently fought any reform that would require extra time and effort.

Perspectives on Reform: 'We Need to Change the Way We Do Business' vs. 'It's Just Another Passing Fad'

The Idea Team

The Good Old Boys' and the Idea Team's contrasting notions on whether or not detracking would 'fit with their routine' was based in part on whether they viewed the reform as part of a larger model for whole school change, or whether it was simply another educational innovation which they were being asked to implement. Members of the Idea Team understood that detracking was one of many reforms that needed to happen at the school. They knew that detracking was not going to work in isolation, and in fact had strong beliefs about the accompanying curricular and organizational changes that needed to occur. 'We need to change the way we do business', stated a teacher. In this regard, they had an understanding of the complex nature of school reform.

First and foremost, the Idea Team recognized the need to overhaul Central's curriculum along with detracking. Early on, the committee of teachers discussing heterogeneous grouping was working separately from the committee discussing the curriculum. Idea Team member Barbara Cooper commented on this: 'Why doesn't the Heterogeneous Grouping [Committee] get together with the Curriculum [Committee]?

Because I truly believe the dilemma they are faced with is that they are looking at a traditional curriculum. You can't detrack a traditional curriculum'. She realized that detracking in the subject-specific, traditional curriculum was unworkable because the traditional curriculum was not suited for classrooms comprised of students with varied prior achievement levels. Bilingual education teacher, David Walker, concurred, arguing that not only did the curriculum need to change, but in addition teachers needed to learn new pedagogy for teaching heterogeneous groups: 'I think we really need help in order to learn not just strategies, but I think specifically lessons that are content specific, that empower the teachers to deliver curriculum and instruction to the students regardless of their skill level'.

In addition to the necessary curricular changes for detracking, Idea Team teachers cited two key complementary organizational features of the restructuring plan: the house model of organization and team teaching. An Idea Team teacher argued the benefits of the house model by stating: 'We could give kids a smaller community of teachers who know the kids and who can communicate and provide a structure of support'. Another teacher reiterated: 'We could have some ownership of these students because we see them more than just one period in our class'.

Similarly, math teacher Gail Cummins reflected on how the house and team teaching model would help a broader range students: 'I teach a group of freshmen this year. These are the kids that need the fact that I talk to their English teacher and their science teacher. They need that connection, even if it's just four teachers'. Ms Cummins had been a teacher in the CLA program and had experienced the benefits of a close collaboration with other teachers first hand. Another teacher, who had not been part of CLA, imagined the potential benefits of team teaching: 'I just notice even when I do that informally, and I talk to my students, and I say, "well I understand that in Biology you're having a difficult time or you're doing real well in this part". When students know that teachers are talking and are concerned . . . that's going to be a big help'.

In addition to believing that team teaching would be beneficial for the students, Idea Team teachers embraced the notion of a school structure which would allow them more opportunities for collaboration with each other. As one teacher explained: 'I don't think that individual teachers are necessarily the best ones to make decisions, but when we get together as a group we really work things out'. According to the Idea Team teachers, teamwork would help them make the school a better place for their students.

The Idea Team teachers, particularly the women members, also saw a restructured school as a potentially nurturing place for each other. In part for this reason, they sought team teaching and collaborative working relationships. Employing a metaphor of caring, the Idea Team women often discussed the support they provided for each other in creating and implementing the restructuring plan. This included sharing responsibilities of attending meetings. Teacher Amy Darren, explaining her relationship with another teacher in her department, Donna Burton, stated: 'I'll be there for her and she'll be there for me, and we'll tell each other about what happened'. According to another teacher, the Idea Team women also served as sources of emotional support for each other during difficult times of the reform process: 'What sustains us when we lose hope is the knowledge that there are other people we can lean on'. She then added: 'We cry on each other's shoulders and then we come out and go for it again'.

In fact, the statements by Idea Team teachers about their relationships with each other are consistent with gender studies of school leadership. Feminist attributional research on women administrators points out that a focus on relationships and establishing a sense of community are important elements to women's work in schools (Regan, 1995; Restine, 1993; Shakeshaft and Perry, 1995). Gilligan (1982) summarizes women's concerns about relationships as an 'ethic of care'. In some ways, the importance which the Idea Team placed on collaboration and forming houses where both students and teachers would have stronger connections might have been more a function of their socialization as women and less as teachers.

Overall, the Idea Team teachers recognized that the traditional departmentalized secondary school structure and curriculum isolated them from each other and that this fragmentation had negative consequences both for their students and for themselves as professionals. By restructuring the school into smaller houses where teachers worked in teams, they hoped that their contact with each other would be increased, which in turn would improve student achievement.

The Good Old Boys

In sharp contrast to the Idea Team, the Good Old Boys' efforts were directed toward maintaining the traditional structure and culture of the school, including tracking and the pro-tracking ideology. While the Good Old Boys were resistant to reform, they were not resisters as defined by Neo-Marxist resistance theorists (e.g., Willis, 1977) because they were in fact defenders of the status quo and the dominant ideology, not resistant to it. They disagreed with the Idea Team members on the basic premise that the school was not serving all students well. Instead, the Good Old Boys believed that they as teachers, and the school itself, were doing a fine job of educating students. This comment by one of the Good Old Boys is illustrative of this viewpoint:

> I think as a whole our faculty does a very good job, which is one of the problems I had with a lot of the restructuring ideas from the very beginning. They started out with the premise that the job was not getting done at this school. I looked around, and I was very satisfied with the job I was doing . . . I wouldn't mind if my two sons came to this school.

When asked whether restructuring was something he wanted, another Good Old Boy reiterated, 'I was content with the old way of things'.

What school reform meant to the Good Old Boys was very different from what it meant to the Idea Team. While the Idea Team sought to radically transform schooling and fundamentally to change the way 'they do business', the Good Old Boys shared the viewpoint that restructuring was 'another passing fad'. A teacher explained: 'I've been here twenty-four years and I've seen a lot of programs come and go . . . They all go back to the same basic reading, writing, and arithmetic and it comes back to levels where you belong'. An Advanced Placement Spanish teacher, Gil Artiles, concurred: 'This state is changing so fast that nothing stays long enough to really do any good. I've never seen so many programs implemented and dumped so quick'.

The Good Old Boys also saw themselves as a stable force in the school. As a Good Old Boy explained, 'For the great majority of us, this is our job. We've seen the principals come and go, and we've seen the new ideas come and go, and you deal with them as they arise. Deal with the problems. It's your job'. Reflecting upon his tenure at the school, another teacher explained, 'the Good Old Boys kept it all together'. The Good Old Boys saw themselves as carrying the school through potentially destabilizing forces: the turnovers in leadership and the various waves of reform.

Some of the Good Old Boys were also critical of what they saw as very vague restructuring plans on the part of the Idea Team. As science teacher Walter Brown explained: 'We talked about these reforms on that grandiose school level, but I haven't seen anything that I can really sink my teeth into. They talk about this houses thing. Nobody seems to have any idea what in the heck that means. I think there are a lot of things that are sort of vague generalizations'. Similarly, another Good

Old Boy described this faction as thinking in more 'practical' terms than the teachers pushing reform: 'You're going to have to prove the worth of your idea to this group in order for them to start using it'. A social studies teacher reiterated, 'I don't mind doing the dog and pony show if there is a reason for doing it'. Another Good Old Boy explained his view: 'When you use the term Good Old Boys, I get the feeling that you're talking about someone who is dead set against any new idea that comes along. But that is definitely not the case'. Rather, he argued that his faction needed to believe there was a good reason for reform.

Unlike the Idea Team who embraced the notion of detracking in the context of whole school restructuring, the Good Old Boys viewed detracking as an isolated reform, and did not see detracking as being implemented within the context of other mutually supportive changes at the school. Thus it was not surprising that they saw detracking as untenable. As Oakes and Wells (1996) have stated, when detracking is not considered in the context of other mutually supportive technical, normative, and political changes in a school, it has little chance of success. Therefore, the Good Old Boys' actions in defending the status quo were not only rooted in their ideologies, but were simply a function of their commitment to their 'standard operating procedures', as one Good Old Boy stated.

Summary Remarks About the Ideologies of the Good Old Boys and the Idea Team

Members of the Idea Team shared common conceptions of ability, their role as teachers, and the need for reform at Central. For these teachers, the problems at Central lay within the traditional school structure and culture, not within the students. These teachers agreed that all students could learn and the role of the teacher was to provide opportunities in the classroom for all students to excel. The Idea Team sought equity for students (and perhaps for themselves) because they believed that the current distribution of resources only advantaged those in high track classes. Thus, the Idea Team sought to fundamentally transform what 'school' meant with an innovative structure that included detracking and a nurturing, supportive school culture where all teachers believed that all students could learn.

On the other hand, the Good Old Boys' ideology was simply inconsistent with the notion of reform. Instead, their ideology served to maintain the power relations inherent in the school's structure and culture. The Good Old Boys' representation of the school reflected such an ideology: they sought to preserve the notion of the traditional

American high school, complete with tracking, outdated teaching practices, and patriarchal norms.

Clearly the Good Old Boys did not understand the complex nature of detracking reform — or perhaps they did, and realized that their traditional practices would not fit in well in a restructured school. While the above statements give insight into the Good Old Boys' ideologies about education, their statements also point to their insecurity and lack of efficacy. While they shared a common set of beliefs about education, much of the Good Old Boys' resistance to detracking can be attributed to an unwillingness to change and a fear of what a disruption in the current structure might mean for them. Undoubtedly, the Good Old Boys feared losing their long-established power and status in the school, as well as changing their practices. Although it is a little less obvious with the Idea Team, it is likely that they too were partially motivated by self-interest in that they stood to gain power and status at Central if their school-wide restructuring plan was instituted.

> *How Ideological Consensus Developed: Critical Inquiry*
> *and Collaboration vs. The Daily Rituals of Coaches*
> *with Union Ties*

That teachers within each faction shared remarkably common goals and strong ideological consensus is quite interesting, given that each group represented teachers from a wide variety of disciplines. Usually, it is within departments that teachers share the most ideological similarities (McLaughlin et al., 1990; Siskin, 1994). Of course a distinct possibility is that the ideological differences of these groups bifurcated by gender is rooted in their socialization and life experiences as men and women. We know that gender strongly plays into the teaching profession as a whole, and therefore influences teachers' ideologies (Acker, 1995; Apple, 1994). However, while gender may be the basis of their ideological similarities, especially with regards to the role of the teacher and attitudes towards collaboration, gender also played a strong role in shaping the political positions and maneuverings of each group in reform (as is the subject of the next chapter). Meanwhile, the actual processes and within-group interactions through which each group achieved ideological consensus is also important, and is detailed below.

The Idea Team

Besides discussing how the Idea Team's ideologies were rooted in their life and teaching experiences, we must also assess the role of critical inquiry in leading to the group's consensus on issues of reform. Sirotnik and Oakes (1986) assert that 'through a methodology of critical reflection, a theory of the school can be built which provides an understanding of why things are what they are, how they got that way, and whose interests are being served by the current conditions' (p. 81). Several other notable social theorists have emphasized the importance of teachers inquiring into the inequities inherent in the current system, and have pointed to the role of critical inquiry in shaping teachers' ideologies (Giroux and McLaren, 1986; Gramsci, 1971; Kanpol, 1992; Sirotnik and Oakes, 1986).

In fact, there was evidence to suggest that the Idea Team teachers at Central jointly engaged in a critical inquiry process concurrent with the development of the original restructuring plan. It seems that as the Idea Team teachers fleshed out the elements of reform, they began to see how tracking perpetuated the existing social structure. As English teacher Lucy Berg remarked, 'we've got to get away from thinking that students belong in slots'. Betty Allen, a member of the Idea Team, also explained:

> We need to start thinking about the students and the parents and the people we serve and in the larger sense of the world . . . We can see the turmoil and the strife [in] the world and who better than a group of people who deal with the academic education [of students]? . . . Who better to create an internal world structure that should be the model for the external world?

Engaging in a critical inquiry process seems to have enlightened teachers on the relationship of school sorting practices to the larger social structure and culture. In the process of inquiry, the Idea Team appears to have explored the problematic culture of tracking, not simply the structure: they deconstructed the pro-tracking ideology.

More generally, the fact that the Idea Team teachers (and the CLA teachers) were part of a collaborative sub-culture likely contributed to the productivity of their critical inquiry process and their consensus about reform. In collaborative cultures, working relationships between teachers tend to be spontaneous, voluntary, development-oriented, pervasive across time and space, and unpredictable (Hargreaves, 1994). Certainly the Idea Team characteristics fit this description: teachers voluntarily joined together from various departments due to a genuine interest in reforming the school and providing students with greater access to a quality education.

However, while the Idea Team themselves achieved consensus around reform through their own collaborative culture, they were an island in a school which was more accurately described as 'balkanized' in which like-minded teachers grouped together in some unproductive ways (Hargreaves, 1994). While the participation in self-reference groups can support innovation, it can also fuel discontent and retrenchment (Nias, in press), as we see in the next section on the Good Old Boys.

The Good Old Boys

The Good Old Boys had a strong sense of self-identification and were mutually supportive of one another. The Good Old Boys had powerful consensus on most issues related to education: when I asked the Good Old Boys if they shared common beliefs and values the answer was always 'yes'. The Good Old Boys' consensus was based in their common defense of the status quo. Unlike the Idea Team, this consensus did not develop through critical reflection on how their school practices and inequitable societal outcomes were related. However, like the Idea Team, this was a voluntary group who had extensive, regular, albeit informal, opportunities to engage in conversation with each other. For example, despite their lack of popularity with the administration, due to their extra-curricular activities as coaches, most of the Good Old Boys enjoyed the privilege of having the last period of the day free to prepare for team practice. As a Good Old Boy explained: 'I have sixth period prep because I'm involved in golf and I do things after school'.

Moreover, the Good Old Boys had ritual daily meetings in the cafeteria which took place before school and during the morning nutrition period. Women teachers did not take part in these coffee klatches. A Good Old Boy explained this by stating, 'not too many of the female population, persuasion, or whatever it is, even seems to go into the cafeteria to have their coffee plug in the morning or at nutrition'. On the contrary, their daily rituals were looked upon as with disdain by the women teachers. For example, a women teacher described the Good Old Boys as 'the guys who sit in the cafeteria and kind of feed off each other's negativity'. When I asked why this was a mostly male group, one member of the Good Old Boys chuckled, answering, 'I guess we have the bigger mouths'.

The Good Old Boys consensus on their ideologies about education were also impacted by their status as coaches and by their strong union ties. Both sports and the union were strongly tied into the Good Old Boys' self-interest in preserving the status quo, and thus provided common reference points (and defense mechanisms) with which they could judge the reform. The Good Old Boys tended to focus on not whether the reform was good for children academically, but instead how it would impact their allocation of time and their coaching duties. For example, when asked about their opinions of the various reforms being proposed at the school, several of the Good Old Boys discussed the negative impact on athletics or school spirit instead of discussing the impact on student achievement. Discussing the proposed custom calendar, I had this exchange with math teacher, Bill Dalton:

> AD: Instructionally, do you think it's good for the kids?
> BD: . . . Some of the coaches are very upset because they say we have enough trouble trying to get our kids out for a sport, now what are we going to do during the three weeks that they're off?

As this exchange reveals, when I asked whether the custom calendar would be instructionally beneficial for students, Mr Dalton shifted the discourse to athletics. He added: 'Athletics at our school are really hurting, and part of it is the change in the number of Latinos that we have. Besides in soccer, Latinos are not big athletes'. The Good Old Boys were also concerned about what the impending move to a new school site would mean for athletics, as plans did not yet include a swimming pool or a new football stadium. These comments point to the primacy of athletics in the Good Old Boys' notion of what 'school' means.

The role of the teachers' union in shaping the Good Old Boys' ideologies about education was also important. All of the Good Old Boys were strong union supporters. Moreover, one of the Good Old Boys, a math teacher, was the union president. The influence of the union on the Good Old Boys' ideologies was evident both in their emphasis on what was 'fair' for teachers and in their preference for a decision making structure based on majority vote. The Good Old Boys' focus on fairness is illustrated in this statement by the principal: 'There is a need for fairness where all teaching staff have the same number of students and the same number of this and the same number of that'. The union also saw its role as protecting the interests of teachers who were resistant to change. The union president explained: 'If we have ten or twelve people at the school who don't want to do it and complain to us to protect them, then we have to be sure that they have rights, either to transfer to another school where they don't have to do it, or if there are too many of them then we won't sign off on it'.

In sum, unlike the Idea Team whose common ideologies grew in part out of productive discussions about the status quo at their school, the Good Old Boys' ideological consensus resulted from their extended interaction in ritual daily meetings and their common bond as coaches with strong teachers' union ties. In addition to the Idea Team and the

Good Old Boys, also comprising Central's balkanized school culture, there existed the Middle Group, whose isolation from each other led to little ideological consensus around issues of education.

The Middle Group

The 'Middle Group': Remaining Nameless

Although the Idea Team and Good Old Boys were both very vocal about reform, the vast majority of teachers did not ally themselves with either the Idea Team or the Good Old Boys and had little involvement in the politics of the restructuring efforts. This third group, the Middle Group, represented more than half the teachers at Central and comprised teachers from all the departments in the school including math, English, science, social studies, vocational education, foreign language, and bilingual education. The Middle Group also represented the full range of age and experience within Central: some were new teachers to the school; others had been there for ten, fifteen, or twenty years, though there were more new teachers than seasoned veterans. In terms of gender, ethnicity, and track level, the Middle Group broke down along the same lines as Central as a whole. The Middle Group was a diverse lot of teachers.

In keeping with the group's diverse nature and low-profile concerning reform at Central, some teachers referred to the Middle Group as the 'okay' group. However, for the most part, the Middle Group, though acknowledged as distinct from the other two factions, basically remained nameless throughout the course of the reform process. Thus, while the moniker, 'Middle Group' was not widely used, it describes their apolitical, neutral position in reform at Central.[2]

As mentioned, the Middle Group greatly differed from the Good Old Boys or the Idea Team in not being an identifiable faction in political terms. They also did not have, as one teacher stated, 'a label stamped on their foreheads'. In fact, in order to avoid being labeled as reformers or resisters, members of the Middle Group did not share their beliefs about reform publicly. Even though some teachers in the Middle Group participated in discussions of reform at Central, none voiced strong enough opinions to be stigmatized as allying with the Idea Team.

The Middle Group also used passive resistance techniques in the restructuring movement: as one member of the Middle Group noted, their main involvement in reform consisted primarily of 'watching the crossfire' between the other two factions. Although the Middle Group publicly characterized themselves as people who were 'on the fence' about detracking and reform in general, many of them had views, even strong ones, both in favor and against reform. An inquiry into their ideologies reveals that many in the Middle Group shared similar beliefs with both the Idea Team and the Good Old Boys.

The Ideologies of Middle Group Teachers

The Common Bond: 'I Don't Enjoy Politics'

What constituted being a member of the Middle Group was the strong lack of interest, even disdain, for being involved in the micropolitics of the restructuring process at Central. Over and over again, members in the Middle Group expressed this. As one social studies teacher stated: 'I don't necessarily have a lot of patience for the pettiness and the politicking'. An English teacher stated: 'I deliberately stay out of it because I don't like to hear controversy'. As one foreign language teacher simply put it, 'I don't enjoy politics'. In general, the Middle Group were particularly loath to choose sides between the Idea Team and the Good Old Boys. One new teacher stated: 'I try not to concern myself with [the politics]'. Similarly, a veteran math teacher stated: 'I'm too old to mess around with this stuff'. He further elaborated on his dislike for the political infighting at Central by adding: 'If you're going to go argue or have a pissing match with each other, do it someplace else. I don't want to be around it'.

Other Middle Group teachers had more practical and less political reasons for not being involved in restructuring, such as a lack of time. As one social studies teacher explained: 'Honestly I don't always have as much time, because of my other responsibilities, to get involved. . . . [W]hen [you] put teachers together they do everything very slowly. They tend to talk a lot and don't get much done'. Other teachers echoed this by stating: 'It's really hard to be able to put in the extra time', or 'I was just doing too many things' (when the planning for restructuring was taking place).

There were also idiosyncratic reasons for the Middle Group's choice not to get involved in restructuring. For example, an African-American social studies and special education teacher harbored resentment against teachers and the administration for apparently 'having ridiculed [him] for his unorthodox way of teaching'. He was thus irritated when these same teachers asked him for advice on teaching low achieving students. He viewed this as 'ironic'. This teacher was not alone at Central in having personal reasons in making a conscious decision *not* to support either the reformers or the resisters.

The balkanization of Central's faculty also contributed to their lack of involvement in reform efforts. Unlike the Idea Team and the Good Old Boys, who had extensive within-group interaction and collegiality, members of the Middle Group tended to be isolated from one another with little personal or professional interaction. These teachers closed the door to their classrooms and seldom spoke to each other. Many of these isolated teachers taught foreign languages and believed that the proposed reforms had little effect on them. One foreign language teacher expressed this isolation: 'If we have a staff day and I had to decide whom I'm going to have lunch with, I would have to go by myself. I would not feel comfortable joining in with a group or anybody except possibly one of the Spanish teachers'. She then tersely added: 'I don't mix with anybody'. In some ways, the strong personalities and ideologies of the Idea Team and the Good Old Boys forced the Middle Group into an 'out group' status.

Although the Middle Group did not have an active role in the micropolitics of school reform, they did have opinions, strong and often diverse, about what 'school' means, as I explain in the next section.

Conceptions the Role of the Teacher and Reform: 'Let Me Shut the Door and Make the Magic Happen'

In a manner quite similar to the Idea Team, some of the Middle Group voiced great satisfaction in helping traditionally low achieving students experience success in school and viewed this as a wonderful part of their job as teachers. However, in a manner similar to the Good Old Boys, they focused their efforts on their own classrooms, believing that school-wide change was futile. As a social studies teacher stated: 'The most exciting kids to teach are the ESL [English as a Second Language] kids. They still find education really, really exciting and they are the most rewarding to teach'. This teacher had little interest in teaching any other students in the school, certainly not the honors students whom she called 'obnoxious . . . to be honest, because so often their egos get in the way and it takes the fun out of it'.

It should be noted that some members of the Middle Group were rather committed teachers and did not seek boundaries to their teaching lives as the Good Old Boys did. One teacher stated: 'I'm a firm believer in living in the area that you work. You run into [your students] at the grocery store. You run into them at the movies . . . They stop being [your] students and they become [your] friends . . . That's neat'.

On a different note, the professional isolation of many of the Middle Group seemed to affect their ideologies about the role of the teacher. A veteran math teacher explained: 'Give me the kids, let me shut the door and make the magic happen. I like to be left alone. If it's good for kids, then let's do it. If it's good politically, I could care less'. Although this teacher, like the Good Old Boys, felt that ability was relatively fixed, he believed he could play a role in raising students' achievement level, like the Idea Team. He stated: 'I think some youngsters are going to have to start at a level less than college prep, and I think its our job to bring them up to that level'.

Similarly, some Middle Group teachers felt that reform efforts were best targeted at the individual teacher level, rather than at the organizational or curricular aspects of the school. A bilingual education teacher explained: 'We have some really good teachers that really push the kids . . . I try to push the kids, challenge them and I tell them everyday that teachers who don't do this, it's because they don't care'. Like the Idea Team teachers, he felt that more teachers needed to be personally connected with their students: 'There are too few of us doing that'. He added: 'A lot of the students really can't relate to some of the teachers. They just don't see them as people with same mores, just as teachers'. He did not feel this issue could be addressed in the context of structural changes, however; it had to happen with individual teachers.

In sum, many in the Middle Group felt they could make a big difference in the lives of their students and some felt they were already accomplishing this. Yet, unlike the Idea Team, they did not see the politics of school change as worth their effort — they were satisfied with individual achievements in the confines of their own classrooms. Perhaps the Middle Group teachers were simply being politically pragmatic in betting that a restructured Central High School would never become a reality.

Perspectives on Detracking: From 'I Think that it is Needed' to 'I Don't Want the Curriculum Dumbed Down'

Although there was some agreement among the Middle Group on the role of the teacher and the need (or lack thereof) for reform, these teachers had sometimes strong and divergent views on restructuring. I analyze their views on detracking as a case in point. Like the Idea Team teachers, some Middle Group teachers were in favor of detracking and imagined its potential benefits. However, like the Good Old Boys, other Middle Group teachers voiced negative opinions and often skepticism that it would succeed.

On the positive side, there were those Middle Group teachers for whom detracking made sense. Heterogeneous grouping seemed to fit with their conceptions of what a restructured 'school' might mean. However, these opinions were voiced somewhat tentatively. For example, a vocational education teacher stated:

> I haven't gotten a full in-depth view of what is going on with [detracking], but I think that it's needed because as we're looking ahead to the real world where these students are going, they're going to be mixing with different people of the same level or different levels. I think that it's good to start here in the school atmosphere.

Similarly, a social studies teacher agreed about the possible long terms benefits of heterogeneous grouping: 'The sharp kids need to know that there is a big part of the world out there that isn't as smart as they are'. However, she did feel that these initially lower-achieving students might need extra support in order to succeed. Or, as she explained: 'I would rather see an emphasis on making the movement from level to level easier', instead of removing the tracks all together. Also voicing a positive opinion, one music teacher embraced detracking as one of many reforms that needed to happen at Central: 'I think the whole restructuring effort is necessary for the students' sake. I see it providing more opportunities and options for the students'.

Revealing negative, albeit tentative views towards detracking, one teacher stated: 'I don't know what they've actually done with it, but I don't think the top students belong [with other students]'. Another teacher questioned whether detracking made sense, given her experiences in the classroom: 'I think what tends to happen is the slow basic kid tends to group toward himself. The really sharp kid will finally say, "leave me alone and let me do my work, I don't want to be in this group. I don't want to do the work for all these kids"'.

Reminiscent of the comments by the Good Old Boys, a foreign language teacher had a much stronger negative reaction toward detracking:

> When they talk about grouping them heterogeneously which I assume means untracking . . . I know that if it were my child I would pull him out of public school and put him somewhere else . . . I don't want the curriculum dumbed down for him. I don't want him to fit with what I consider to be an element that is so incredibly uneducated.

Her comment is reminiscent of both the Good Old Boys' lack of full understanding about detracking and their belief that (Latino and African-American) students from less well-educated backgrounds did not belong in the same class as (white) college preparatory track students. On the contrary, there were teachers in the Middle Group who resisted the idea that teachers at Central had different goals for students from different racial backgrounds. An English teacher stated: 'I think most teachers are pretty open minded. I think most teachers look at students as students. I don't think whatever ethnic group the students belong to has any bearing on their teaching or any judgments they are going to make about the students'.

In essence, none of the middle group teachers were strongly committed to detracking, and none were interested in joining in the battles on its behalf (either for or against). Some were interested in learning more about it, and thought the end result might be beneficial. Other teachers doubted that it would have positive effects, and some had very strong feelings against detracking. Overall, few teachers in this group appeared to have critically examined the school's tracking practices and the overlaps between race and track placement that pervaded Central.

Summary Remarks About the Middle Group

There was considerable diversity in the ideologies of the teachers who represented the Middle Group in the restructuring at Central High School. While they did not constitute an ideological subculture of like-minded teachers, what they did share was an unwillingness to become active agents in the politics of reform and prefered an isolated professional existence in the balkanized Central school culture. These teachers did not ally with a political self-reference group like the teachers in the Idea Team and Good Old Boys.[3] In order to avoid being pigeon-holed into either the Idea Team or Good Old Boys factions, the Middle Group mostly resisted taking a strong stand for or against restructuring, especially in a public context. Although the Middle Group was not a faction in political terms, and they did not pro-actively impact the course of reform, their role vis-à-vis the political strategizing of the Good Old Boys and the Idea Team was important and is discussed in more detail in the following chapter.

Conclusion

What existed at Central was two factions of teachers — the Idea Team and the Good Old Boys — with starkly different ideologies about what 'school' means, how their role as a teacher was defined, and with strong disagreements about the status quo. The Idea Team, a predomin-antly female group, wanted to radically transform the school, expand and redefine their role as teachers, and emancipate students who had historically been disadvantaged by the system. The Good Old Boys, on the other hand, wanted to preserve the status quo, maintain their traditional role as teachers, and ignore larger issues such as the way in which the track structure at Central perpetuated societal inequalities. A third group of teachers, who represented almost half the faculty at Central, the Middle Group, comprised members with ideologies rang-ing in similarity to teachers in both factions, but who stayed out of the political crossfire between the two sides, and to this extent, were mostly non-committal towards reform or the status quo.

Given what we know about the contrasting group identities and ideologies of the Good Old Boys and the Idea Team, we can see why in the Fall of 1992 with the Idea Team suggesting major restructuring at Central, the Good Old Boys would be outspoken and react strongly against these reforms. In fact, assistant principal Betty Allen forebodingly predicted: 'There is a Good Old Boys syndrome here that is fighting harder than ever'. We now turn to a discussion of the heart of this book: the intersection of gender, micropolitics, and reform.

Notes

1   The term *faction* is used to describe groups who compete for dominance. As such, factional rivalry is a zero-sum game in which the losers are likely to be resentful, even vengeful (Lande, 1977).
2   I use the term the 'Middle Group', which is what one teacher at Central called this group, for simplicity's sake.
3   Some of these teachers looked to their departments for self-identification, although this was not uniformly true.

4   The Competition over what 'School' Means at Central

At Central, the Good Old Boys and the Idea Team competed over whose definition of the school would win out — the status quo or a school dramatically recultured and restructured. Despite the strong reform efforts of the Idea Team, the Good Old Boys captured the dominant representation of the school by attacking their opponents through crass gender politics, thereby preserving the traditional structure of the school and the patriarchal culture that accompanied it. This is the story of how it happened.

This chapter is organized both to illuminate the sexist discourse used by teachers at Central in the politics of representation as well as to show the sequence of political action at Central. The chapter begins with a discussion of the patriarchal school culture that existed at Central before the restructuring efforts began.

The Patriarchal School Culture and the Power of the Good Old Boys

In the second chapter, I mentioned that the school culture of Central could be characterized as patriarchal, in which masculine norms of behavior prevailed over feminine. I define patriarchy according to Adrienne Rich's (1979) broader definition:

> By [patriarchy] I mean to imply not simply the tracing of descent through the father . . . but any kind of group organization in which males hold dominant power and determine what part females shall and shall not play, and in which capabilities assigned to women are relegated generally to the mystical and aesthetic and excluded from the practical and political realms. (p. 78)[1]

At Central there had long been an entrenched hierarchy of men over women, in which the Good Old Boys' informally ruled Central and held the power to define what 'school' meant. Math teacher, Gail Cummins mentioned a symbolic example of the historic patriarchy at Central:

'When I first started [ten years ago] I was hired as math/science teacher, and I was the only woman in the science department. As far as getting materials, they were locked in somebody's cabinet [presumably one of the Good Old Boys]'. She added: 'I had no access to them'. Consciously or not, teachers at Central employed norms in the course of their interaction that reflected gender relations on the societal level. Again, this was not surprising at Central as teachers are part of a society where gender is an important principle of social differentiation (Cunnison, 1989).

Although this structural element of subordination was less apparent at the school in the 1990s because more women teachers had joined the school, Central continued to be known as a generally difficult place for women teachers. Women were not only denied access to the informal power structure (e.g., they were silenced by men in faculty meetings, and they did not enjoy the Good Old Boys' informal connections to the school board), they were also historically labeled as aggressive when they did assert themselves. As a male teacher commented, 'I'm the chairman of a department that is very feisty . . . all women. I'm the only guy there and they start pushing me around a lot'. According to research on the role of gender in teachers' work lives, this is a classic example of the double bind that women secondary teachers often find themselves in: if they are outspoken, they are labeled aggressive; if they are silent, they are labeled submissive and have no voice (Ball, 1987). As such, the patriarchal school culture at Central High School disempowered women teachers, making them feel as though their contributions to the school as a whole were minimal.

The patriarchal school culture at Central also reflected societal relations of power in a community and larger society in which men were commonly accorded higher status than women. This was especially true in the largely Latino community of Central where gender roles were very traditionally defined. In an interview, a Latina counselor at the school explained the power of patriarchy in the community: 'This father calls me and he says, "Why are you putting those ideas in my daughter's head to go to college? Women don't go to college, they belong in the home having babies and taking care of their men"'. A social studies teacher recounted a similar experience from a student discussion in her classroom: 'We had a discussion . . . about the end of World War II, when the men came back and the women lost the jobs that they had acquired during the war. And guys [in the class] were saying, "Well, yeah, she needs to go home and take care of her kids"'. These incidents point out the power of patriarchy in defining the expectations and relegated status that existed for many young women in the community. Thus, it is not surprising that the Good Old Boys had support for their cause, given the traditional values in the community.

The Good Old Boys, by controlling the definition of the school as 'traditional', maintained the patriarchal culture of Central High School. Since the power resided with these male teachers who were resistant to change, many teachers viewed change in any wholesale way as impossible at Central, even though there were an equal number of 'forward thinking' women teachers. This patriarchal school culture at Central existed without disturbance until restructuring began in 1992. Even with early discussions about change by the Idea Team, there was little genuine threat to Central's existing culture and structure because, as the principal noted, most viewed that '[change] would never happen to Central High School'. In fact, it was only when the school actually received the large restructuring grant from the state that conflict and political organizing began in earnest. However, the collision (and the gender politics) between the Idea Team and the Good Old Boys really began with the CLA program, and it is here that I begin.

Laying the Groundwork for Reform with CLA: 'We can Make a Difference'

The reform-minded agency of the Idea Team teachers had its roots in the development of the Central Lifetime Achievers (CLA) program three years before the restructuring grant was funded. CLA provided the important building blocks for school-wide restructuring. Assistant principal, Betty Allen, discussed this relationship:

> A lot of the groundwork for the restructuring started about three years ago with a few faculty . . . There is a group of about 8 or 10 faculty who really have equal access for students at heart, and they thought that students were slipping through cracks. That group came to the administrative staff then and wanted to try a pilot program that is now called Central Lifetime Achievers (CLA). And that is possibly the forerunner . . . for the ability to change.

The CLA program attempted to change the distribution of resources in the school through a small detracking effort. In creating this program, CLA teachers sought to show the faculty and the community what could happen when formerly low-achieving students were given a chance to excel. Several teachers discussed the excitement and challenge of their original involvement with CLA. Math teacher and Idea Team member Barbara Cooper recalled the speech by the national union leader which led to the development of CLA: 'He said you've got to put your thinking caps on. The public is getting sick of you, the government is sick of you, and its not working'. She described the creation of CLA as a program of unlimited opportunities and amazing potential:

> I was one of those teachers who sat down and just brainstormed, *So what do you think we could do? . . .* We read a lot of Ted Sizer's stuff about what you could do if you grouped kids and all of a sudden came up with what it could look like. And then we went to the faculty and asked for input . . . Then all of a sudden the district said *do it!*

Site and district administrators applauded the fact that Central's own teachers had developed the innovative CLA program from the ground up. Frank Marsh, the assistant superintendent, talked about this example of teacher agency: 'We didn't plant the seed. The strongest teachers stepped forward and said "we can make a difference"'.

The dominance of Central's patriarchal culture was so strong that the above mentioned Idea Team member Ms Cooper, who had spearheaded the creation of CLA, decided not to teach in CLA for fear of political reprisals. As Ms Cooper explained: '[As math] department chairman, I thought if I taught in [CLA], I would dilute my power because I would become one of "[the reformers]"'. Interestingly, two years later, Ms Cooper changed her mind and began to teach math in the CLA program. As she defiantly explained: 'To heck with political power. This is where I want to be and I am going to do it!'. As Barbara Cooper's comments and actions point out, teacher agents at must not only come up with the reform, but even more importantly, they must be prepared to defend their political decisions against the current structure and culture, even in the face of political retribution. Although Ms Cooper eventually taught in the CLA program, Central's dominating patriarchal culture had an incredible chilling effect on teacher involvement in a reform that sought to upset the status quo.

Notwithstanding the above, the CLA program at Central represented a first major breakthrough for teacher agency in reform at Central. However, the creation of CLA also triggered a strong defense of the power structure by the Good Old Boys. At this point, the Good Old Boys couched their attack in terms of their resentment towards CLA teachers for the so-called 'special privileges' given to those teachers by the district in the form of extra preparation time and smaller class sizes. A Good Old Boy (and science teacher) stated:

[CLA] was just kind of implemented from above. Well, there was a small group of teachers in favor of it. A lot of us felt like it took resources away from the rest of the programs. Those teachers only had four [classes] instead of five . . . The faculty really wasn't behind it . . . It made naysayers out of a lot of people.

The Good Old Boys viewed the CLA program as simply the opening salvo in the struggle over bigger issues, most especially the status quo and their protection of it. As one Good Old Boy stated in this regard: 'This CLA program is a total farce . . . That was supposed to be a program that lasted for a few years. Well what they ended up doing was they kept making it larger and larger!'.[2] As this statement shows, even at the early stage of the CLA program, the Good Old Boys' were mobilizing for a full-fledged showdown with the Idea Team.

No doubt, the Good Old Boys felt threatened by the CLA program. The Good Old Boys derogatively referred to CLA as the 'Central Losers Association', as opposed to Central Lifetime Achievers. In order to maintain power over the school from the new viable threat of the CLA program and its teacher developers, the Good Old Boys argued that the presence of CLA had subtracted resources and created additional burdens for them when in fact this was untrue. Since many of the teachers who participated in CLA were also members of the Idea Team, the Good Old Boys saw them all the more as 'one and the same'.

The Creation of the Plan for School-wide Restructuring: 'How Do We Get There From Here?'

The success and the spirit of the CLA program pushed reform-minded teachers to approach site administrators about implementing something like CLA on a school-wide level. The teachers argued, 'if we can teach college prep material in an enriched environment to "standard level" students, why wouldn't that be good for all students?'. While the CLA program laid the groundwork for school wide restructuring, the principal Bob Foster represented an additional essential ingredient for its inception. The removal of the previous principal in 1991 had created low staff morale and little incentive for ambitious changes at Central. As one teacher said, 'having someone come in and say, "I am the leader and I have some real strong beliefs and I'll help find what's best for kids" attracted teachers to jump on the reform bandwagon'. As the most powerful administrator in school, Bob Foster's institutional position greatly facilitated the agency of reform-minded teachers in moving toward school-wide reform. At the beginning, Bob Foster facilitated the agency of these teachers in fulfilling their goal of comprehensive reform by having the power and the courage to invite the entire school community to develop the vision for a new Central High School.

According to English teacher and Idea Team member Lucy Berg, the plan for restructuring Central High School started with a very broad discussion organized around three big questions: 'What do we want our graduate to look like in the year 2000? What does the school look like that will produce that graduate of the year 2000? And how do we get there?' In an informal manner, teachers and school officials broke into small groups and brainstormed with butcher block paper and markers in a large room at Central High School. It was after this initial meeting that the Idea Team was formed. The Idea Team then met for a series of days and reformulated the brainstorming on the Central graduate of the year 2000 into a vision statement. As Lucy Berg pointed out, the vision statement was a loose assembly of ideas from various groups on how to achieve that vision. Lucy Berg, Barbara Cooper, assistant principal Betty Allen, and a third female teacher who since left the school, then turned the Idea Team's vision into a seventeen-page proposal for restructuring, which subsequently received funding from the state department of education.

Due to the vague and unbounded nature of the vision for the restructuring plan, the writers of the proposal had a fair amount of latitude in establishing its contents. They decided to maximize the potential of the restructuring plan. For example, according to Lucy Berg, detracking became a part of the restructuring plan as a natural interpretation of the vision of 'how we would be able to do these things for *all* kids'. Ms Berg conceded that the proposal might not have represented the opinions of the group of fifty, much less the entire faculty.

In fact, many of the Good Old Boys were upset that the plan was not reflective of their ideas. They argued that the restructuring plan had been created 'subversively' by a small group of people (the Idea Team) and supported by the administration. This statement by a long-time science teacher (and Good Old Boy) illustrates their viewpoint:

> Even the way this thing got started was on the wrong foot. First of all, they had a meeting at the beginning of the year, on a Saturday. And they said, 'Well, we invited everybody'. Well, not everybody can come on a Saturday. And a lot of people didn't come. And a lot of people felt like, wait a minute, you know we're not in on this.

A few of the Good Old Boys, however, had to admit that they could have been involved had they been interested. Social studies teacher

Peter Owen explained: 'The principal tried to get me on the Idea Team. I begged off that'. Math teacher and union president Bill Dalton also agreed that his input on the plan would have been accepted, but he chose not to get involved because, as he explained, 'I can't spread myself that thin'.

The Defense of the Status Quo: 'A Full House Assault'

After the restructuring proposal was funded, the Good Old Boys quickly labeled the Idea Team as 'the ones responsible for all this stuff we're going to have to do'. Uncomfortable with this perception, the Idea Team asked the principal, Bob Foster, to orally present the plan to the faculty, even though he was not part of the Idea Team nor one of the grant writers. Immediately, he too became associated with the restructuring plan. During the principal's presentation, the Good Old Boys became very angry about what the proposal asked them to do, especially with respect to detracking. As teacher Lucy Berg described, 'there was a full house assault on Bob Foster' by these teachers. While Bob Foster stated that the plan was a 'blueprint that was open to negotiation', the perception among the Good Old Boys was, 'it's theirs and not ours'. In other words, the restructuring was purely the product of a 'a small group of people', namely the Idea Team.

In their attack of the restructuring plan, the Good Old Boys argued that the restructuring was 'grant driven' — they now had to do what the Idea Team proposed, regardless of whether or not there was consensus on the reform, because money had to be spent. This angered the Good Old Boys because, in the words of math teacher Ralph Boskey, '[They] didn't have a buy in on this'. He added: 'Don't tell me this is the way it's going to be because that's the way it is on a sheet of paper'.

During the Good Old Boys' attack, the Idea Team teachers fell into the background, and did not come to the rescue of Bob Foster and take ownership of the plan they had themselves developed. The following statement by Lucy Berg embodies the group's discomfort in defending their proposal and explains their decision to let the male principal take the heat:

> I hoped this was going to be a one time thing and that people just wanted to have somebody to point at . . . and I felt Mr Foster had to stand there and take it. It's his job . . . Okay, this is not something that was his idea, but still he can speak for it. And at that point having other people stand up there would have made the rest of us targets.

Another teacher on the Idea Team viewed the Good Old Boys' venting of their frustrations as cathartic and beneficial to the restructuring process: The Good Old Boys had now spent their negative energy and would henceforth acquiesce to the reforms. (As it turned out, this was not the last they heard from the Good Old Boys.)

On the other hand, Assistant Principal Betty Allen, who was out sick the day of the restructuring plan presentation, was very frustrated with the Idea Team's decision not to defend their ideas, particularly since Ms Allen and the Idea Team had met for several hours before the fateful meeting in order to prepare a defense for their proposal. As Ms Allen described her exchange with the Idea Team teachers after that day: '[An Idea Team teacher] said, "it came on so fast and we didn't really know what our role was". I said, "what have we just spent two hours doing? Preparing to respond to questions as an Idea Team. That was your role!" '. Moreover, Ms Allen was also upset that the Idea Team had hung the principal, Bob Foster, out to dry.

As mentioned, given the patriarchal culture which existed at Central, it is not surprising that members of the Idea Team, especially the four women who wrote the grant, were uncomfortable defending themselves. Additionally, these teachers likely found it difficult to defend their political choices in the face of their colleagues because of the powerful hegemony of the pro-tracking ideology. Therefore, they relied upon the political leadership of their male principal, Bob Foster, who they felt was in a 'safer' position to take the heat. Reform at Central clearly required much more than the inspiration for distributive justice and the willingness to learn and try new strategies. It required teachers to do something they had never done before: make the difficult choices to work against the current structure and culture, in this case tracking and a culture of patriarchy, and defend this choice before their faculty peers.

The culture of patriarchy greatly affected the Idea Team's reaction to the first showdown with the Good Old Boys. For example, although Betty Allen, was much more involved than the principal in developing the proposal for restructuring, once the grant was funded, like the Idea Team teachers during the lambasting of the principal, she fell into the background, placing the future of reform in Bob Foster's hands. Ms Allen assumed that Mr Foster as a man would have more success in communicating the ideas of the reform. Thus, Betty Allen, almost overnight became the 'woman behind the man'. In fact, coincidentally and ironically, she subsequently left in the second year of reform to assume a position as principal at another high school.

Importantly, the Idea Team members were not alone in being silent or silenced while the Good Old Boys actively and angrily spoke out against the restructuring proposal. The Middle Group, the majority of the attendants at the meeting, resisted taking a strong position on the plan. The Idea Team left the fateful meeting concerned that real change could not happen unless the Middle Group bought into change as well. An Idea Team teacher remarked: 'A few people are doing a lot of the work and we need to get buy in and support from more people. We need them to speak out'. Bob Foster was also concerned that the Middle Group would thwart reform with passive resistance techniques: 'I will not allow [this] group of people to divorce themselves from the process, and then at the last minute step in, and say "well, because of this and this and this, we're not going to do that" '. That isn't going to happen. And if we can't control that part of it, then I don't think we can move ahead on the restructuring'.

Yet, the passive resistance by the Middle Group seemed rather pervasive and deep-seated at this stage. The Idea Team realized this, and as is explained in the next section, hoped to reach out for support from the Middle Group and even the Good Old Boys whose support was now no doubt essential to the restructuring efforts at Central.

From Idea Team to Facilitating Team: 'Is it a Steering Committee? A Doing Committee?'

After the fateful day when Bob Foster was lambasted, the Idea Team struggled to redefine their role. Betty Allen described their dilemma that during the grant writing process the name 'Idea Team' served a very useful purpose to brainstorm general ideas of where Central ought to be headed. However, with the Idea Team's struggle to redefine itself, Ms Allen questioned the group's changing identity: 'Is it still an Idea Team? Is it a steering committee? Is it a doing committee? What is it?' The Idea Team decided that their new role would be as a steering committee and that they should call themselves the 'Facilitating Team'.[3] The change in name symbolized the Idea Team's shifting identity from a group that generated ideas to a group that hoped to facilitate change. Still, the 'Idea Team' moniker remained with these teachers.

The Facilitating Team hoped to coach individual committee discussions and also, as a team, to serve as a sounding board for committee proposals before ideas were presented to the entire faculty. Their role, as Idea Team member Helen Morris, explained, was to 'meet once a month and talk about what is going on in the committees, how the whole restructuring plan is moving forward, and [deal with] budget and staffing issues'. Their main role, however, was to lead the numerous faculty committees which addressed the issues raised in the restructuring proposal, including the curriculum, the custom calendar, heterogeneous grouping, professional development, assessment, houses, and technology. The committees met at various times: including lunch, after school, and on designated staff development days. The majority of the teachers in the school, including the Good Old Boys and the Middle Group, initially joined at least one committee; some teachers even joined several committees.

While the Idea Team's name and identity was changing, the largest group in the school, the Middle Group, remained true to its passive nature. These teachers described themselves as 'resistant to the pressure to take sides' with either of the two factions. In fact, most of Middle Group signed up to participate in the committees. The involvement of teachers from the Middle Group in the restructuring committees did result in a much larger number of teachers participating, albeit passively in some cases, in discussions about restructuring. Other teachers unwillingly sat through discussions. As one teacher stated: 'When we have a staff development day for [restructuring], my feeling is my God, what can I do to pass the time, because it is so unbelievably boring. It seems to be such a waste of time'. She added: 'And there are others like myself who just sit back and say nothing. Say nothing and do nothing'. And finally, there were a number of teachers who persisted in never becoming involved, even in the discussions about restructuring.

The Good Old Boys also signed up to participate in the various committees. However, some of the Good Old Boys expressed anger that their input was rebuffed by the Idea Team. They claimed that their suggestions were viewed by the Idea Team members as a 'fundamental rejection of what the restructuring grant is all about'. In the committees, the Good Old Boys continued to attempt to exert control, often for fear of change.

However, at the end of the first year of restructuring, Idea Team teachers reported that the general climate at the school had slowly evolved to a point where more teachers felt comfortable voicing their opinions, a condition which undoubtedly rattled the patriarchal status quo long preserved by the Good Old Boys. This was perhaps due to the committee structure, which allowed the voices of more people to be heard in smaller contexts, and due to the increasing power of a new group, the Idea Team. Members of the Middle Group even began to speak up by the end of the first year of reform. One teacher explained: 'We have had conversations like no other conversations that have existed in 22 years that I have been here'. Several teachers commented that for the first time they had informal discussions about teaching and learning.

Moreover, with the change in structure from large faculty meetings, where teachers did not feel safe expressing themselves, to smaller committees with Idea Team teachers as the leaders, the Idea Team teachers began to take ownership of their ideas. For example, when one of the Good Old Boys complained that the administration was 'shoving the proposal down their throats', members of the Idea Team stood up and protested. One teacher defiantly stood up and defended the proposal as her work: 'I've put in 32 hours of my own time developing that proposal (with a number of other teachers) . . . That proposal was my idea!' This assertive behavior was obviously in sharp contrast to long standing traditions at Central and constituted a direct challenge to the hegemony of the Good Old Boys. Central was gradually moving towards more inclusive norms of interaction, which allowed for greater participation of the faculty, not just the loud voices of the Good Old Boys.

The Ineffectiveness of the Restructuring Committees: 'Maybe it's the Kind of Task that a Committee isn't Best Suited to Undertake'

While the committee structure functioned to create more democratic participation in reform at Central and to lessen the control of the Good Old Boys, the substance of what occurred in these groups was not always immediately productive. An interesting case in point was the 'heterogeneous grouping' committee. The leader of this committee, Idea Team member Dan Waters, talked about his attempt to create a group in which productive discussions about detracking would take place. Mr Waters for example, even encouraged some teachers to, as he stated, 'promote the status quo' in their discussions of detracking. Waters explained: 'We ought to have a very vital dialogue about that, and the teachers ought to feel that engaging in a dialogue will have positive results'.

Unfortunately, discussions in the heterogeneous grouping committee meetings did not go this way. Instead, dialogue among teachers was impeded by poor interpersonal dynamics. There was little or no trust among group members, which included members of the Idea Team, the Good Old Boys, and the Middle Group. When a system by which each teacher read and reported on a set of articles — the 'jigsaw method' — was proposed for covering the thirty-two research articles on heterogeneous grouping, members of the group did not trust one another to present the main points of each article in an unbiased manner. Therefore the decision was made that each teacher would read every article.

However, this decision was ill-fated as most teachers simply did not have enough time to do all the reading. Instead, many resorted to simply airing their uninformed opinions on the issue, while a select few reported on the research they had read. Not surprisingly, this resulted in rather unproductive and heated discussions.

Eventually, the heterogeneous grouping committee dissolved, yielding no results, except for ill will on the part of some teachers. Some attributed the dissolution of the committee to Mr Waters' inability to manage the unruly group's discussion in a productive way. Mr Waters thought instead that perhaps it was the nature of the task: 'Maybe its the kind of a task that a committee isn't well suited to undertake'. Possibly the heterogeneous committee was unproductive because this group was characterized by 'contrived collegiality', as it was administratively regulated, compulsory, implementation-oriented, fixed in time and space, and predictable (Hargreaves, 1994). Collaboration among teachers that has these characteristics does not generally lead to meaningful change; this certainly was the case with the heterogeneous grouping committee.

The Idea Team Attempts Departmental Change: 'The Committee was not Going to Have Any Say Anyhow'

In the end, the Idea Team members were not able to make many substantive changes in reform through the committee structure. Some Idea Team members, however, were able to accomplish curricular changes within their subject departments. For example, Idea Team member Lucy Berg, after realizing the inaction of the heterogeneous committee, looked to the English department as a forum for her ideas. According to Ms Berg, 'in a Machiavellian way [the heterogeneous grouping committee] was not going to have any say anyhow'. Thus, she abandoned the heterogeneous grouping committee and moved to the English department as her forum for advocating detracking.

Thus, although the ineffectiveness in the heterogeneous grouping committee thwarted the development of a school-wide detracking plan, the Idea Team teachers were able to move several departments forward in increasing access for students. This move also had the net effect of involving more teachers from the Middle Group in the process of change. The curricular changes were not without a fight from the Good Old Boys, as the battleground moved to individual departments. I now briefly discuss the efforts at detracking in several departments: science, English, and math.

Science

In the science department, Keith Evans, an Idea Team member, influenced his colleagues to move towards providing all students access to a quality science education. He felt proud that this plan came out of his department, but he indicated that his ideas of increasing access came from his experience as a member of both the Idea Team and the heterogeneous grouping committee.

Evans described the development of the curriculum as evolving from several group discussions among members of the department. In planning for this curriculum, the science teachers came to realize that offering all students a quality science education would require a redistribution of resources. The department chair Fred Korn (of the Middle Group) explained:

> Traditionally the non-college prep kids were given the less effective teachers, they were given no equipment, they were given poor quality rooms. I think those issues were much more constricting on them than the psychological label of 'you are not college prep'.

Thus, in the Spring of 1993, the science department developed a creative plan for providing all students access to a rigorous integrated science curriculum. In essence, classes would have multi-age, heterogeneous groupings and would be lab-based, rather than homogeneously grouping students in classes relying primarily on textbooks. After completing two core courses, students could take biology, chemistry, or physics (and then Advanced Placement courses in those areas).

There were three or four dissenting teachers in the department who only agreed to the plan in order to avoid a school-wide restructuring plan. Additionally, these dissenting teachers, including Good Old Boy Norm Shiro, agreed to approve the plan if they did not have to teach the integrated science courses themselves. If they could continue teaching traditional biology and chemistry to eleventh and twelfth graders, they would not block the rest of the department's desire to teach integrated science courses.

The science department's new curriculum was implemented beginning in the Fall of 1993. At the end of the first year of implementation, several of the science teachers cited problems. Notably, teachers of the integrated science level 1 class felt that their students still did not have the tools to succeed in integrated science level 2. Thus, basic level science classes were re-introduced the following year.

English

The English department was also inspired to change its curriculum by members of the Idea Team, and by the fact that the science department had just presented their proposed new curriculum. As the restructuring coach explained: 'When science was willing to do it (and science is nearly all male and English is solidly female), there was sort of a "well, wait minute, if these guys can do this, we can do it too"'. Like the science department chair, the English department chair and Idea Team member Donna Burton, also felt that ownership of the plan was very important to the teachers in her department. She stated: 'It was an open atmosphere. People felt comfortable saying what they really felt'.

The English department planned a challenging course of study that would allow more students access to college preparatory courses through a beginning skill development course that emphasized writing. However, like in the science department, although the English depart-ment came to a consensus on the new curriculum, there were some dissenting voices, and Advanced Placement and honors course were still offered to appease these teachers.

The English department implemented the new curriculum in the Fall of 1993. Some teachers reported that the curricular changes had been positive. However, as in science, the English teachers decided that students exiting the skill development class were not ready for a college preparatory English class. As a result, at the end of the first year of implementation, teachers decided to recreate several sections of a low track English class.

Math

Barbara Cooper, a member the Idea Team and chair of the math depart-ment, attempted to bring about detracking in math through the imple-mentation of a university-developed, thematic, activity-based mathemat-ics curriculum that blended algebra, geometry, and trigonometry over a three-year course of study. All of the integrated math classes satisfied university entrance requirements and accommodated heterogeneous grouping of students.

While she succeeded in gaining consensus to offer several sections of integrated math Ms Cooper was not able to convince the entire depart-ment to move to the integrated program. Thus, the traditional sequence (including standard, college prep, and honors levels) still existed along side this program. Students self-selected into integrated or traditional math sequences. Furthermore, the extra prep period of integrated math teachers during the first year provoked resentment from the traditional program teachers in their department. A Good Old Boy in the department complained about the unfairness of Barbara Cooper's extra period of release time: 'I believe it's for selfish reasons when you have a department chairman that for the past eight years has never taught a full schedule . . . [because she teaches] whatever new programs come down the pipe. . . . And that makes people on the staff bitter'.

Given that the traditional math teachers felt no impetus to change, and that there was strong support for the traditional math curriculum by parents, it appeared that the efforts of the Idea Team in math were unlikely to bring about integrated math and heterogeneous grouping across the board. Thus, the prospects of further reform in math were bleak.

In sum, although there were some curricular changes in English, science, and math, tracking still existed in all departments. Honors and some low track classes remained in all departments, appeasing the Good Old Boys and other teachers who would otherwise have been vehemently against any heterogeneous grouping of students. Nevertheless, the fact that the Idea Team teachers were somewhat more successful at bringing about change within existing structures (departments) is significant, and in fact consistent with Antonio Gramsci's strategy for social change (Gramsci, 1971). Gramsci argues that change must be brought about on the 'basic cleavages' in which people live their daily lives: in secondary schools, this means the level of the subject department (McLaughlin et al., 1990; Siskin, 1994). Perhaps teachers, particularly those in the Middle Group, felt safer expressing their ideas and working toward solutions within departmental subcultures.

Gender Divisions Take Hold: 'It is Divided Sexually in the School'

By the middle of the second year of reform, the Good Old Boys felt threatened by their apparent loss of informal control. After all, some curricular changes had taken hold, there was discussion of implementing a custom calendar, and more teachers had gained the power to speak. Betty Allen explained how the Good Old Boys responded to these challenges to the status quo:

> [The Good Old Boys] have lost some of that power because the movement is happening in spite of them. As a result they are more

entrenched and vocal and have started some pretty dirty tactics. It gets down to malicious gossip now. Then it gets down to some real personal hurts from one staff member to another.

Similarly, a male science teacher, new to the school, explained the dialogue between the Good Old Boys and the Idea Team in faculty meetings as changing from 'healthy disagreement' to 'somewhat vindictive and personalized' to finally, 'belligerent and unprofessional'.

In their effort to defend the status quo at the school, the Good Old Boys targeted their derisive, sexist comments towards eight women Idea Team members who were most actively involved in the reform. They referred to this group derogatively as the 'Dream Team', denigrating the seriousness and feasibility of their reform efforts. Many of the negative references to the Dream Team referred to their alliance with and support from Central's principal, Bob Foster. Good Old Boy Bob Russo believed that the 'Dream Team goes along with everything principal wants to do'. Similarly, another Good Old Boy derogatively referred to the Idea Team as the 'Butt Kissers' again alluding to their relationship with Mr Foster. Clearly, the Good Old Boys were threatened by the Idea Team's position in the school as the 'innovative elite' (Hargreaves et al., 1996).

Teacher Ralph Boskey explained the Good Old Boys' oppositional behavior to the Idea Team by arguing that the Dream Team (a.k.a., Idea Team) had created a culture of teacher factions. According to Mr Boskey, 'The Dream Team assumes that if you're not with them then you have to be against them'. Members of the Idea Team strongly disagreed that they or their restructuring plan had motivated political action from the Good Old Boys. An Idea Team teacher stated that, on the contrary, '[The Idea Team] get[s] all the heat'.

By the middle of the second year of reform, the factionalism at Central High School had clearly developed along gender lines. A teacher, uninvolved in the battle, summarized the gender political strategy of the Good Old Boys as resulting from the fact that the Idea Team did not have 'enough men involved and [the Good Old Boys] started seeing the [the Idea Team] leadership group as being too powerful and making all the decisions'. Bob Foster also viewed reform as divided along gender lines: 'The staff is pretty much divided by gender. And almost without exception, the women are really positive and are really good teachers, and the men are a little more reactionary'. A male science teacher, new to Central, contrasted Central's rigid gender divisions with his last school: '[At Central] the males tend to hang out with the males and the females tend to hang out by themselves, especially certain groups of females.

The other schools I've been at, for the most part it wasn't nearly as pronounced as it is here'.

Even members of the Idea Team were amazed at the direct correlation of gender to agency in reform. As one Idea Team member put it, 'the Idea Team was about two-thirds women at one point. The naysaying group is more male too. That's an interesting dynamic'. As the restructuring coach, Joan Dawson, quickly summed up, 'The majority of the changers are women and the majority of resisters are men. . . . I think it's an attitude'.

Given the stark gender divisions between the reformers and the resisters, faculty inside the school and people outside the school quickly commented on this sharp dichotomy of gender in reform efforts at Central.[4] District administrators, board members, as well as several parents whom I interviewed, were aware of the gender politics in the faculty. In the following section, I describe the specific nature of the Good Old Boys' strategic use of a sexist discourse in derailing reform.

The Good Old Boy's Strategic Use of a Sexist Discourse

In their effort to preserve the status quo at the school, the Good Old Boys resorted to a sexist discourse instead of challenging the women teachers on ideological grounds. To this end, the Good Old Boys sought to undermine the authority and control of the Idea Team women by attacking them on several gendered fronts. The Good Old Boys defined these women teachers as less committed to their jobs. They also argued that the proposed reforms were 'women's work'. Finally, they made sexist jokes about the women in public contexts.

Of the three mentioned gender fronts, the use of sexist jokes was the most pervasive and crass tactic used by the Good Old Boys. According to Cunnison (1989), gender joking is 'men defining women at work in sexual, domestic, or maternal terms, terms which detract from their image as professionals' (p. 166). Gender joking is often used by male teachers to control and subordinate women teachers (ibid.). Moreover, the 'stereotype of the woman teacher is used to pass judgment on women teachers' commitment, competence, and confidence' (ibid.). Like the male teachers in Cunnison's study, the Good Old Boys at Central made jokes focusing on domesticity and femininity that associate teachers with stereotypical definitions of women as less competent and less committed to their jobs.

An exchange between one of the researchers and science teacher Norm Shiro illustrates how the Good Old Boys used a sexist discourse to define the Idea Team women as teachers whose jobs were less important and who had less as stake:

NS: . . . The first thing that pops into my mind is the term 'Cadillac Liberal'.

Q: Could you talk about that?

NS: There are several members of the [Idea Team] whose husbands are well off and sometimes other faculty members get the idea that they may be teaching as a hobby.

Q: Maybe they're not as financially vested in teaching?

NS: As far as my family goes, this is our main source of income. This is *the* job and because of that I look at it from more of a practical standpoint. There's one faculty member who takes a year off every three or four years to revitalize herself or whatever.

Adding insult to injury, he defined the Idea Team women as 'itinerant teachers' who 'weren't the solid backbone of the school'. His statements are reminiscent of Sikes et al.'s (1985) finding that women teachers are often seen as working for 'pin money'.

Good Old Boy Ralph Boskey similarly doubted the commitment of the Idea Team women by decrying one woman teacher on the Idea Team as acting only in her own self-interest. He stated: 'I'm not saying she's not a good teacher . . . I'm simply saying that if you ask people about her they'll say, "well, if she's involved in it what's in it for her?" '. He explained that the Good Old Boys' feelings towards her were in fact personal and had resulted from many years of bad experiences working with her. In this instance, Boskey attributed the Good Old Boy's negative attitude toward restructuring to the so-called bad behavior of one woman on the Idea Team.

At several points, the Good Old Boys demeaned women as professionals by talking about them in patriarchal terms. For example, in an interview, Good Old Boy Norm Shiro, asked, 'who's the gal from UCLA who is supposed to be the guru on heterogeneous grouping?'. When the interviewer explained that it was Jeannie Oakes, he added: 'Quite frankly, she didn't have an answer for some of the questions we presented her with, as far as detracking and some of the practical problems we saw arising from the whole idea'. Given the patriarchal culture of Central and the stereotypical gender biases of the Good Old Boys, one wonders whether a male 'detracking guru' might have been more favorably received at Central.

In order to define the women teachers as less committed to their jobs, the Good Old Boys also defined them in domestic, as opposed to professional terms. According to Idea Team members, the Good Old Boys had seized the teachers' cafeteria as a forum for their highly sexist discourse and jokes about domesticity. As Idea Team teacher Marlene Winters explained, the Good Old Boys sat in the faculty room, reading the newspaper, and 'as women walk by, they say "big butt" under their breath'. Lucy Berg explained the situation in more detail:

> It makes it very hard to work when [women] won't go to the faculty cafeteria unless they're with someone else. They won't go alone because [the Good Old Boys] have set up a long table along the center [and] sort of take it over . . . It reminds you of the athletes' table. Everybody sits down and chows down on steaks before they go crash heads in the big game . . . [And, they make] remarks . . . like, 'men, we're hunters and we're providers and women, they're knitters and cookers and all this' . . . saying this stuff seriously. [They also] accuse the principal of surrounding himself with too many women.

The Idea Team recognized that the Good Old Boys' were using a sexist discourse as a strategy to attack the reform. As Lucy Berg explained, 'They use all sorts of tactics, the tactic of choice, the tactic of the moment, the one which happens to work'. In the case of Central, Lucy Berg is referring to the Good Old Boys' criticizing the Idea Team and restructuring efforts through sexist jokes and innuendo.

The Good Old Boys also demeaned the Idea Team by defining elements of the restructuring plan reform as 'women's work'. Criticizing the house model of school organization, one Good Old Boy stated:

> The problem that I had was that they wanted to turn education back into the little one room schoolhouse. They wanted to have little small core groups and little bitty teachers and then the students married onto the teacher and carried on with them [throughout high school].

Likewise, another Good Old Boy referred to restructuring as 'all those little group things'. Norm Shiro minimized the importance of what the Idea Team was working on as something that had simply 'caught their fancy'.

In the Good Old Boys' critique of the reform as 'women's work', Ralph Boskey attacked a new 'traditional' math curriculum his department had adopted on the specific basis that it was developed by women. He prefaced his comments on this by stating: 'I'm getting gender based, but that's the way it goes in life'. Boskey immediately focused on the fact that 'women developers [are] behind this [the new math curriculum]'. As I interviewed Mr Boskey, he proceeded to read the list of developers from the teachers' manual and counted the number of women on it. After doing this, he told me that 'Fifteen [woman teachers] out of . . . [counts again] . . . twenty-seven [developed this curriculum] . . . My problem . . . is the writers of this thing . . . didn't like a traditional set up'. He then added: '[The new system] doesn't create as much pressure for the girls in their classes and for them as teachers. It doesn't create as much pressure for them to be the sage on the stage'. When asked whether other teachers agreed with his overall criticisms of the math curriculum, Boskey answered, 'I hate to say this, but there is a gentleman down the hall who agrees with me'.

By defining the reform in terms of 'women's work', the Good Old Boys undermined both the credibility of the women as teachers and the importance of their efforts. As another example of the disproportionate use of gender politics as technique to critique the restructuring movement and the Idea Team women, most conversations about reform quickly turned to gender discourse no matter where the conversation started. The following dialogue between a female interviewer on the research team and one of the Good Old Boys, Peter Owen, illustrates this:

Q: What reforms are being pushed right now that you find particularly problematic?

PO: There is no way in hell I would be a homeroom teacher. [This is the] day and age of woman simply being able to say . . . 'Well, I can bring a sexual harassment suit against them [the male teacher] any time I want.' . . . You [the female interviewer] could make a sexual harassment case against me. I have no witnesses. I have no leg to stand on. The way it's written right now, I'm dead meat . . . [With] tutoring, I have to be careful that I don't sit in the room with *a* female because anybody . . . can make a claim against me. And that's a sad ass commentary on society, but that's the way it is. I'm not going to be . . . part of a house routine where they're going to tell me I'm going to be locked in with a group of kids for four years and some girl comes into puberty and decides that I'm her dream idol. God knows whatever sick [reason] she'd have to think that I would be even remotely interested in her.

Here, the female interviewer raised a discussion about school restructuring and the teacher shifted the conversation to the terrain of gender, arguing that a homeroom period would put him in jeopardy of a sexual harassment lawsuit. This Good Old Boy's argument against a restructuring reform is obviously far removed from educational discourse.

That the Good Old Boys employed a sexist discourse instead of taking on the Idea Team teachers on ideological grounds reveals the defensive strategy used by this entrenched group in the politics of representation. For the Good Old Boys, the women teachers were an easy target. They could fall back on stereotypical gender roles that reinforce male power in society instead of constructing a sound educational argument against the reform efforts of the women teachers. Cunnison (1989) argues that 'the practice of assessing one another by stereotypical gender roles is so deeply embedded in our society that it pervades most social situations, including those of work, regardless of whether it is formally appropriate' (p. 152). Perhaps the Good Old Boys feared that if they directly challenged the Idea Team on ideological grounds by attacking specific features of the reform, their unwillingness to change their ineffective ways of teaching might have been exposed.

The Discourse of the Idea Team Women: 'We Know What's Best for Kids'

Interestingly, the Idea Team adopted a gender discourse themselves in order to rebut the sexist talk of the Good Old Boys. The shifting of discourse from education to gender had the ironic effect for the Idea Team members of deflecting attention away from the importance and validity of their restructuring efforts at Central to what became a pure micropolitical battle fought on gender lines. As the Idea Team mounted their own gender political attack (albeit not as crass) against the Good Old Boys, their energy for pushing such reforms as detracking and houses was waning. In this regard, the Idea Team had unconsciously shifted the venue of reform to the Good Old Boys' home turf: raw power politics at Central.

First, the Idea Team defended their position by shifting their discourse to the terrain of 'we know what's best for kids'. Due to their gender socialization, the Idea Team claimed that women teachers were the proper choice for leading school reform. As Idea Team teacher Barbara Cooper argued, women teachers were uniquely poised to handle reform:

Women are moms. They run the household. They do laundry. They cook. They do everything. We [women teachers] are used to handling more. Men, they don't have that nesting instinct. For men, or for husbands, [teaching] is a job that they do from 8 to 3.

She explained that men were not accustomed to doing many things at once, which school reform required, and were not as well suited for the caretaking aspects that being a mother (and a good teacher) required. Ms Cooper added: 'There are men who do . . . but we [women] do everything'. She then asked me about my own husband, and stated: 'I'm sure he's a terrific husband, but let's face it, men just don't do as much as we do'. Of course these defenses led the Idea Team right into the Good Old Boys' trap, as they had been arguing all along that women were best suited to be caretakers — not competent teachers, however.

Other Idea Team teachers also gloated about the fact that women were simply better suited to lead a reform effort than men. As one female math teacher said, '[change is] risky, and women have a better support network than men. [Women teachers] have more conversations back and forth . . . The guys haven't quite figured out that it is okay to go to somebody and say "this activity didn't work, what did you do?"'. Another Idea Team teacher succinctly summed up that 'women on this campus are better writers . . . [and] better at formulating their ideas'.

In this same vein, the Idea Team women attacked the Good Old Boys for not wanting to commit the time that restructuring required. A teacher explained: 'It's a lot easier to open the filing cabinet and pull out the same old, same old'. The Idea Team portrayed the Good Old Boys as lazy and uninterested in their students. One Idea Team teacher remarked on this concerning the social studies department:

> It's run by a very efficient organized woman . . . It's hard for [her] to get all those people [Good Old Boys] to come to a meeting. They're [mostly] coaches . . . One's about ready to retire [and] . . . teaches the standard track . . . [One day, a female student] came into my room in tears because for her final exam in American History he had them copy the glossary. And, she said, 'Ms Berg, I know I'm better than that'.

Just as the Good Old Boys undermined the authority of the Idea Team by defining them 'itinerant teachers', the Idea Team defined the Good Old Boys as more concerned with coaching than teaching, biding their time until retirement, and as wholly uninterested in their students.

In an unusual twist, the gender politics at Central reached a climax when in elevating their defense to a new level, several of the Idea Team women teachers filed sexual harassment suits against several of the Good Old Boys, charging them for episodes that dated back several years. As Marlene Winters, one of the teachers who filed a harassment suit, explained: 'I ha[ve] five pages single spaced . . . since 1987 . . . [of] stuff that is sexually harassing'.

During one of my visits to Central, at the end of the second year of reform, Bob Foster related to me the origins of a recent sexual harassment suit: in their typical manner, one of the Good Old Boys was vulgarizing about a woman teacher behind her back. However, what was new to Central was that this woman teacher was going to press sexual harassment charges against that Good Old Boy. At the end of the second year of reform, threats of sexual harassment suits were proliferating in an unprecedented manner at Central. Bob Foster conjectured that the rise in the number of lawsuits was a combination of the Good Old Boys trying to reassert their patriarchal domination of women teachers, and of these women finally getting the courage to hold the Good Old Boys accountable for this inappropriate behavior. Mr Foster viewed the lawsuits as extremely significant in the struggle for power among the two groups of teachers. He even optimistically believed that if the women teachers kept this up 'they [would] have a real strong possibility of taking things over themselves'.

The main purpose of the harassment suits for the Idea Team was to put an end to Central's patriarchal culture that had allowed unpleasant and demeaning gender discourse to be waged with immunity against women teachers for years. (In fact, the Idea Team members were less interested in punishing specific men).[5] Certainly, as Bob Foster had suggested, the fact that Idea Team members were at last speaking up heralded to some degree a shift in power at Central from the Good Old Boys to the Idea Team. However, arguably, more importantly, these harassment suits fully deflected the attention of everyone in the school — most especially the main reformers, the Idea Team — away from reform. And, as will be seen, this became part of restructuring's downfall at Central.

What about the Middle Group?

Although the Middle Group was on the sidelines for the micropolitical battles between the Good Old Boys and the Idea Team, they quickly surmised the gendered elements of it, though with varying viewpoints on the situation. A veteran male teacher (but not part of the Good Old Boy faction) neutrally characterized the micropolitics as 'pretty much some female teachers against some of the old boy male teachers'. Similarly, another male teacher (also not part of the Good Old Boy faction) had a detached view of the battle over the reform: 'I would say that the factions pulled in different directions. . . . The unofficial power group [the Good Old Boys] [finally] said . . . no way [to the restructuring plans]'.

This teacher viewed most of the dissent as coming from one Good Old Boy, Bill Dalton, who was president of Central's powerful teachers' union.

Some teachers in the Middle Group, however, were initially mobilized against the Good Old Boys by the filing of the sexual harassment suits by the Idea Team. As the restructuring coach explained: '[Teachers in Middle Group] would walk into the teachers' lounge and overhear some dirty joke and turn to [the Good Old Boys] and say, "That is completely inappropriate. I am tired of hearing you do that in this room. I want you to stop"'. For a short period of time, some members of the Middle Group were cognizant and proactive in getting the Good Old Boys to stop their demeaning gender discourse, helping to put an end to gender joking in the staff room.

The Good Old Boys' Diverse Political Strategies: 'Creating Doubts' and 'Rabble Rousing'

Although the filing of sexual harassment suits and the support of the Middle Group momentarily put an end to the sexist jokes, it did not end the struggle between the Good Old Boys and the Idea Team. Bob Foster realized that conflict had to be resolved among the teachers on-site at Central in order to reduce the possibility of the Good Old Boys resorting to outside political forces to accomplish their goal of maintaining the status quo in the school. Therefore, in the middle of the second year of reform, with conflict between the Good Old Boys and the Idea Team at an all-time high, the principal hired a conflict management consultant to help create better norms for communication among the two factions.

Unfortunately, Bob Foster's efforts at conflict management did not stem the Good Old Boys from engaging in political organizing outside the school. The Good Old Boys immediately reached out for support among parents and the teachers' union. In particular, they used their alliance with a school board member, Bill Bathgate (the former principal at Central when most of them were hired years back), to convey negative impressions about the Idea Team's restructuring efforts to board members. Finally, as the principal feared, the Good Old Boys went directly to the district superintendent to complain about the restructuring efforts at Central. In the final section of this chapter, I describe in more detail the dramatic methods and consequences of the Good Old Boys' political maneuverings to stop the Idea Team and their reform efforts.

Rallying Parents Against the Custom Calendar

Interestingly, the major battleground in the community over reforms at Central did not involve the more radical detracking plan but the custom calendar, a feature of the restructuring plan which 80 per cent of the faculty, including some of Good Old Boys, supported in a vote. Good Old Boy Bob Russo, a physical education teacher and the self-described 'biggest rabble rouser on campus', orchestrated a major community effort against the custom calendar. Mr Russo employed his connections with the school board and with parents in the community in order to stave off the calendar change. Just before the calendar was to be presented to the school board, Mr Russo began campaigning negatively against it in his classrooms and with parents in the community (primarily parents of white honors students). Mr Russo rallied a large group of parents to speak at a school board meeting against the calendar. Parents argued that the calendar would increase gang problems and curb students' opportunities in the summer.

In response, the Idea Team and Mr Foster tried to garner community support for the calendar and presented research on the educational benefits of the custom calendar to the school board. In the end, the board sided with Mr Russo and the affluent parents he had rallied and, after a series of heated meetings, voted against the calendar. One teacher expressed amazement and disgust at how such a small group had curried favor with the school board: 'There were probably eight or nine nay-sayers. But, they were heard repeatedly by the board . . . [They had] an incredible control of that situation'.

Mr Foster was also extremely exasperated by what happened with the custom calendar: 'We spent a year giving them . . . information . . . on how it would help the vast majority of students here at Central High School . . . and every time they would say, "well what about [x] . . ." It was like they kept moving the target'. Tom Baxter, an assistant principal, commented that the custom calendar, though not a redistributive policy on its face, became a symbol of liberal ideology, an example of a larger movement to 'take away from the haves and give to the have-nots'.

The custom calendar issue testifies to the power of a single teacher's agency in bringing about change or, in Mr Russo's case, hindering change. This corresponds quite well with social theory that says, although all agents have some degree of power, domination exists when there are asymmetries of resources employed in sustaining relations of power (Giddens, 1979). In this case, the asymmetry of resources came from the raw power of the affluent parents who enabled the agency of

Mr Russo to prevail over the Idea Team, notwithstanding the latter's better academic arguments on the benefits of the custom calendar.

Adding insult to the injury of the Idea Team's defeat on this reform, although Mr Russo had mounted his attack on the custom calendar with the affluent parents on educational grounds, Mr Russo's actual reasons (which he shared in confidence) were much more pedestrian and self-interested. As Mr Russo put it, 'I'm the water polo coach and the swimming coach. My kids [both his students and his son who was joining Central the coming year] won't get vacations. In water polo, they'll have to practice during breaks . . . Not with my kid here . . . is the [custom calendar] going to happen'. Moreover, in Mr Russo's mind, there was no doubt who was responsible for the proposal of this reform: '[The notion of a custom calendar] is dreams. And that's why [the proponents of the reform] are called . . . the "Dream Team" '.

Through the Superintendent's Back Door

The involvement of Central's superintendent, Rich Beaufort, affected reform and was essential to the Good Old Boys' efforts to retain the political control of Central. Mr Beaufort was a close friend of influential school board member Bill Bathgate and a sympathetic ear to the Good Old Boys' concerns. Arguably, Mr Beaufort became unfairly biased in favor of the Good Old Boys' positions on reform before hearing the Idea Team's perspectives. As such, the superintendent became a thorn in the side of the Idea Team. The differential treatment by the superintendent was illustrated when three women on the Idea Team attempted to directly approach the superintendent to suggest a change to the school day schedule, which would allow more time for teacher collaboration. Mr Beaufort gave the Idea Team teachers a very negative reception, vetoed their plan, and told them he would only deal directly with Mr Foster on policy issues. He later scolded Foster by saying, '[your] staff . . . is out of control'.

Unlike the Idea Team members, the Good Old Boys did not have to go through the normal channels to air their grievances. As Idea Team member Keith Evans related on the incident involving the three women who went to see the superintendent, '[our] group is treated as a hostile group. Yet [the Good Old Boys] go over to the superintendent's door any time they want and complain'. Because of the Good Old Boys' personal connections with school board and the district office, such access was available to them. Bob Foster placed the source of some of the Good Old Boys' power on Mr Beaufort's shoulders: '[He] is empowering [them] as long as he allows them to come in the back door and moan and bitch'.

The superintendent not only erected political barriers against the Idea Team in terms of preferential access and treatment for the Good Old Boys, he also endorsed structural barriers that limited the time that teachers (primarily the Idea Team members) had for teacher collaboration. In the first year of reform, the district office had approved the Idea Team's plan to make the school day longer so that every other Friday they could take a half day for meetings and staff development. However, in the second year, the district office eliminated this schedule, relying on the Good Old Boys' opinion that it was a bad idea. As a result, the Idea Team no longer had a designated time in which to collaborate on issues related to restructuring. In this regard, the superintendent, through structural means, facilitated the agency of the Good Old Boys and constrained the agency of the Idea Team.

The Final Blow

At the end of the second year of reform, the final blow to restructuring efforts at Central occurred: Bob Foster, the school's reform-minded principal, resigned. As will be seen, Bob Foster's resignation, both practically and philosophically, marked the end of restructuring at Central. However, there are many theories on why Foster resigned. Bob Foster himself told me that the Good Old Boys' strategic use of gender politics, their unwillingness to change, and their political connections outside the school, particularly with the superintendent, had succeeded in creating an impossible climate for reform. Since he only wished to stay at Central if he could push the school forward, he resigned.

The Idea Team teachers, obviously very frustrated and upset, also immediately pointed the finger at the Good Old Boys and their personal and professional connections with Mr Bathgate and Mr Beaufort. Several Idea Team members told me that Mr Foster had ostensibly been fired. Adding to this theory, allegedly, Good Old Boy Bill Dalton, the teachers' union president, had circulated a petition of 'no confidence' against Foster and had garnered the necessary number of signatures to at least bring Foster's termination in front of the school board. It should be noted that apparently this petition was never brought before the board because Mr Foster resigned beforehand.

Another theory surrounding Mr Foster's resignation involved allegations that the Good Old Boys had spread rumors questioning Mr Foster's motives in pushing for reform at Central. According to Good Old Boy rabble-rouser Bob Russo, Mr Foster was using the reform efforts to create a name for himself as a star principal. Mr Russo told me, 'somebody wants to [build] a resume'. Good Old Boy Norm Shiro argued that 'a lot of what has been going on in the name of restructuring has been to satisfy the egos of some of the administrators and certain faculty members. The student, as usual, has been left out of it'. To this end, although Mr Foster was writing an EdD dissertation on school finance, the Good Old Boys circulated a rumor that Bob Foster was writing a dissertation on the successful implementation of restructuring at Central and thus needed this to happen in order to get his degree.

There was also speculation that Bill Bathgate, the powerful veteran board member, had been a major facilitator of Mr Foster's resignation. Given Mr Bathgate's close personal ties with the Good Old Boys, he viewed Mr Foster's downfall as based on Mr Foster's own foolhardy actions concerning the Good Old Boys. As Mr Bathgate put it, 'If a Good Old Boy wanted to do something . . . I would have tried to have met those needs'. Mr Bathgate was also unabashed in explaining that because of their involvement in community-supported extracurricular activities, the Good Old Boys had considerable power within the district: 'The band man has power. The football coach [a Good Old Boy] has power'. He explained that there is a 'large constituency of parents' who support the Good Old Boys and will address the school board on their behalf of their actions. Moreover, Bathgate suggested that Mr Foster was extremely naive in thinking that he could just ignore the interests of the Good Old Boys and completely ally himself with 'the Dreamers', as he called the Idea Team, given the vast differences in power of the two groups in the community.

Irrespective of the reason for Bob Foster's resignation, overnight, the Idea Team had lost their main administrative sponsor for restructuring. The Idea Team, though active agents in reform, relied upon the principal to 'go to bat for them' both in and outside the school. The Idea Team applauded Mr Foster's leadership, especially his willingness to try to remove hurdles for them. Bob Foster's resignation took the steam out of the Idea Team and symbolized the Good Old Boys' victory in the restructuring battle. The Good Old Boys had fought for Mr Foster's removal and they had succeeded. The turnover in administration at Central represented the deathknell of reform at the school.[6] After Bob Foster's resignation, representatives from the state department of education visited Central to speak with teachers and administrators and then withdrew funding for one year while the school 'got their act together'. Mr Foster's successor as principal, Tasha Davis, decided not to reapply for restructuring funding. In fact, Idea Team teachers stated that

Ms Davis, a long time community member, chose to focus her efforts on building the school's athletic teams and instituting programmatic efforts for at-risk students, rather than addressing student improvement through school-wide reform. In the end, the Good Old Boys had won the war for the definition of the school, with the demise of detracking efforts and the maintenance of traditional schooling practices.

The Aftermath of Reform at Central

With the end of restructuring and its funding and a new principal at Central, tensions between the Good Old Boys and Idea Team members appeared to have dissipated. Most teachers attributed the lack of tension between the groups to the removal of restructuring funding. As one of the teachers from the Middle Group wisely reflected, 'The reality is that restructuring for us was divisive'. Still, beneath less tense relations, resentment was harbored by members of both factions. As Idea Team member Ms Cooper stated: 'There are still some men in the school who hate my guts'.

Some teachers at Central felt the move to the new school site, (which occurred eighteen months after the restructuring funding was removed) with its departments organized into separate, subject-centered school buildings, had lessened interaction among faculty subgroups, and thus eased some tension (and lessened collaboration) between faculty. As Good Old Boy Ralph Boskey explained, '[Given our new] campus, there are [some] people on this campus I haven't even seen this year. People I would see in the morning or at lunch or coffee, I don't see . . . anymore. [The new school design] has broken up a lot of networks'.

I had a similar impression when I returned to the school for follow-up research two years after the end of the restructuring effort. I discovered that neither the Good Old Boys nor the Idea Team was a driving political force. Neither group had a unified presence on campus. In fact, several prominent members of both factions were physically not there. A couple of Idea Team members had left the school for teaching positions elsewhere. One of the Good Old Boys, Bill Dalton, the influential teachers' union leader, had retired. Several Good Old Boys were away on sabbatical. Several teachers told me that the Good Old Boys were a less powerful force on campus.

This was also certainly true of the Idea Team. As several Idea Team members told me, the restructuring effort had created a bond that allowed teachers from different departments and backgrounds to come together; without that bond, these teachers mostly worked independently. Just like progressive-minded teachers in the Middle Group, many Idea Team members were now focusing on the quality of their teaching in their own classrooms and not on school-wide issues. In some ways, this more isolated nature was unsurprising given the highly emotional and charged impact of the internecine fighting with the Good Old Boys over restructuring. As one Idea Team member stated, 'Those of us who were involved in it are not going to go and stick our necks out anymore'. Although this same teacher viewed this outcome as sad, he accepted the reality that whole school change was never going to happen at Central High School.

Conclusion

As this chapter describes, the reform process, at least for some time, disrupted the hegemony of the Good Old Boys as Idea Team teachers gained the power to voice their opinions. As the Good Old Boys began losing their power and control over the school, they resorted to crass gender politics, making derogatory comments about the women teachers (the Idea Team members) involved in reform, in attempt to undermine the reformers' authority and control. The Good Old Boys' use of a sexist discourse against individual female teachers, instead of constructing sound educational or intellectual arguments against the proposed reforms, reveals the defensive strategy used by this entrenched group in the politics of representing the school. The women teachers were an easy target for the Good Old Boys given the strong stereotypical gender roles supported at the school and in the community and society at large. Idea Team teachers, adopting the gender discourse themselves, retaliated by defending themselves as women and by filing sexual harassment suits against several of the Good Old Boys.

Earlier in this book, I had proposed that reform-minded teachers have to defend their political choices, as detracking reforms challenge strong societal beliefs about race, intelligence, and meritocracy. However, interestingly, in the case of Central High School, these were not the beliefs that the Idea Team teachers had to ultimately defend in their push for detracking at Central. Instead, they had to defend their position as women.

While the filing of the law suits was a dramatic and momentarily powerful step on the part of the Idea Team, gaining the support, for a short time, of the teachers in the Middle Group, the Good Old Boys succeeded in shifting the focus of the discourse from educational reform to gender politics. By effectively coopting the discourse and defining the reform and the reformers in gendered terms, the Good Old Boys successfully won the contest over whose meaning of 'school' would prevail. When the attempt to dominate by one group over another is successful, a hierarchy of meaning is formed in which one of the ways of representing the world gains primacy over others (Mehan, 1990). In other words, the Good Old Boys succeeded in preserving the traditional structure of the school and the patriarchal culture that accompanied it.

Moreover, it is not surprising that the Good Old Boys were successful in their attempts to garner support for the maintenance of the status quo in the school, as their meaning of the school was strongly reinforced in the very traditional and patriarchal structure and culture existing outside the school, both by district administrators and with parents in the community. Couching the issue as political choice between the traditional male Good Old Boys and the progressive female Idea Team rather than about the merits of the restructuring reforms, the Good Old Boys were on powerful terrain with their strong political network which comprised the power in the community and in the district.

I now turn to the gender politics of reform at two other restructuring secondary schools for a comparison with Central.

Notes

1   Rich's definition of patriarchy was also used by Weiler (1988).
2   In fact, the CLA program was phased out in 1993, as the teachers hoped the entire school would move to a similar model — the restructuring plan they had proposed. This did not occur.
3   For the sake of simplicity, I continue to refer to this group as the 'Idea Team'.
4   Several of the men and women teachers considered the issue of why there are more women involved in change efforts than men. A woman teacher on the Idea Team explained that sometimes a male teacher would join a committee and then say, 'how come there are so few men on this committee?' This discouraged some men from participating.
5   Literature on sexual harassment claims suggest two principal reasons for them: to force the man to change his behavior or to make him an example by which other men will relearn the boundaries of appropriate behavior (Mann, 1994).
6   On the contrary, some teachers suggested that Betty Allen was the 'brains behind the reform' and that restructuring fell apart when she left the school. In fact, it truly fell apart when Foster resigned.

5 Common and Diverging Themes in the Gender Politics of Educational Change

Reflecting upon the gender politics of reform at Central High School, the school's restructuring coach remarked: 'This situation is not unlike most high schools I know. It just happens to be more intense'. This chapter uses data from two other schools in the larger detracking study, Explorer Middle School and Grant High School, to describe how gender politics play out in reform efforts within vastly different school contexts. The data from these schools are compared to the findings of the Central High School case. Briefly, like the Good Old Boys at Central, male teachers at Explorer and Grant led the traditional camps of teachers. In this regard, gender was a salient feature of the politics of representing what 'school' means at Explorer and Grant. However, at neither of the two comparison schools did the gender politics escalate to such a degree as to overthrow the reform efforts altogether, which occurred at Central.

This chapter begins with a discussion of the reform efforts and gender politics at Explorer Middle School, followed by a discussion of Grant High School. I conclude this chapter with a comparison of the gender politics at these two schools to Central High School, highlighting the common and diverging themes that exist across the three schools.

Explorer Middle School

A Brief Overview

Explorer Middle School is located in the downtown area of a northwestern United States city. During the period of our study, the school served a population of approximately 550 students in grades six through eight. Thirty per cent of the students were American Indian/Alaska Native, 64 per cent were white, and the remaining 6 per cent were Latino, Asian-American, or African-American students.[1] The white population was overwhelmingly middle income while the Native American population was largely low income.[2]

A major issue within the school and the district as a whole was the low achievement of Native students. Native students failed at a much higher rate than white students and were grossly underrepresented in the gifted program and over-represented in special education at the school. Many Native students were identified as 'communication disordered', referring to their perceived lack of vocabulary and their discomfort in expressing themselves verbally. In addition, teachers, administrators, and students reported that some teachers treated Native students poorly. There was also concern about the lack of representation of curricula pertinent to Natives.

Explorer became a middle school in the early 1980s when the district adopted the Carnegie Turning Points middle school model for its two junior high schools. Before implementing the middle school model, the district encouraged teachers to explore the research on middle schools and their own philosophies about educating early adolescents. After this initial period of research and soul-searching, teachers were given the option to transfer to elementary or high schools if they were uncomfortable with the shift to the middle school model of organization. If they chose to stay in one of the new middle schools, teachers were given extensive training on team teaching, on new instructional techniques, on how to better communicate with parents, and they were given opportunities to attend conferences and visit other middle schools. The teachers who stayed at Explorer Middle School felt as though this process allowed them to attain the buy-in that was needed to make the middle school model successful. For example, a teacher recalled:

> There was a lot of discussion about the difference between the subject specialist and the non-subject specialist and where people fit into the scheme of things. There was lots of decision making at the grass roots level.

She added: 'There wasn't going to be any cramming down anyone's throat'. In addition, according to the superintendent, the principal at the time believed wholeheartedly in the middle school model, which greatly facilitated the shift.

In keeping with the Carnegie Turning Points model, the district encouraged the school to reduce ability grouping and tracking. However, detracking did not become a movement at Explorer until the principal, Renee Black, joined the school in 1989. She explained: 'When I came, the practice [of detracking] was sort on paper, but not in practice'. She initiated detracking by hand sorting students into classes in order to ensure racial and ability heterogeneity. She also initiated the mainstreaming of both special education and gifted students. Additionally, she hired a number of teachers who supported her vision and removed several teachers who did not. The district supported her vision, with the exception of her stance towards heterogeneously grouping gifted students. However, the lack of district support left her open to attack by the powerful constituency of parents whose children at the school were identified as 'gifted'.

In 1992, in order to facilitate close communication and support among teachers, Ms Black made the decision to alter the teacher team and house structure at the school. Specifically, she modified the traditional middle school model from grade level teams of four or five teachers to smaller teams of two or three teachers across grade levels. Teams of two or three teachers taught all academic subjects to a team of sixty to ninety students. However, the principal did not dictate how teachers taught or how they organized students within teams. Teacher teams were free to organize their time as they saw fit; some maintained heterogeneous grouping across all subjects, while others re-grouped students by ability for certain subjects. In addition, some teachers taught in an interdisciplinary fashion, while others taught single subjects. All teachers in each grade level had a ninety-minute shared planning period each day.

Gender Politics and Ideological Diversity at Explorer Middle School

This new organizational structure divided faculty at Explorer Middle School into two camps of teachers — those in favor of the changes initiated by the principal and those against. Some faculty were rather critical of the principal's approach to reform. For example, as one teacher described: '[After attending a conference], Ms Black got it in her mind that certain things were wonderful . . . The next thing you know: Pow! We have it here . . . In my opinion some of the things have not been healthy'.

The split among the faculty mostly mirrored an ideological division between those teachers who preferred a traditional, departmentalized, junior high structure versus those who supported the child-centered, interdisciplinary middle school model. Teachers also themselves divided along old guard/new guard lines, with the veteran teachers being the more traditional and thus more resistant to the small team structure, and the newer teachers more progressive and in favor of the small teams.

The ideological differences between the two camps were most evident in their views towards heterogeneous grouping: the traditional camp was more comfortable with homogeneous grouping, and the progressive camp was committed to heterogeneous grouping of students. A teacher in the more progressive camp articulated her commitment to heterogeneous grouping in this way: 'I don't know what it would be like if we had four gifted kids together, or four learning disabled kids, or four Native kids, or four white. I just couldn't — I can't see that. That wouldn't be really conducive to learning anything'. Similarly, another woman teacher stated: '[Heterogeneous grouping] offers the low kids as well as the high kids [the chance] to be connected with the same kinds of things . . . And I think that really is the foundation of meeting the needs of all students'. As these comments suggest, to the progressive teachers, heterogeneous grouping simply made sense.

Accordingly, progressive teachers were more likely to see ability as socially constructed. For example, a Native studies teacher argued that the patriarchal white social structure reinforced erroneous beliefs about ability:

> The way I look at it, our country is predominately Western European middle-class and above. It's run by men. It has been forever . . . To me, everybody is gifted and talented . . . It's just that we have people telling us that we're too dumb, too silly, too fat, too dark, too woman, too whatever.

By contrast, traditional teachers tended to view student ability as a fixed, innate quality. Sixth grade teacher Mark Jeffrey's reiteration of his comment to a student in his low-ability math class reveals his conception of student ability: 'I certainly didn't want to say this is the "dummy" class. [I told him,] "you'll struggle this year, but you'll get through it". [I] attempt to encourage [the students] along, but they are aware of [their ability level] too'. Mr Jeffrey added: 'I think one of the strengths of the tracking system or homogeneous grouping is that you can target those types of situations'.

Accordingly, traditional teachers were much more circumspect about whether or not detracking was effective. For example, seventh grade teacher Mr Dawson stated:

> In my opinion, heterogeneous grouping does benefit the low-end kids. But . . . parents complain that their high-end students seem to be not going as fast, and they are used [in the classroom] to . . . bring other kids along. Now you can debate this . . . but I would have to agree that . . . the high-end kids are the ones that benefit the least

from heterogeneous grouping. The middle [range of kids] benefit, and the low benefit, but not the high.

Sixth grade teacher Tim Walker agreed, explaining that his team dealt with this by introducing some homogeneous grouping:

> We have decided that completely heterogeneous just doesn't cut it all the time . . . On our team, the science and the geography is completely heterogeneous, the math and English end up being not quite so heterogeneous. We just need to throw a dose of reality into it. You just can't buy the [principal's] whole program.

Not only did the faculty's preference for reform divide along ideological lines, but also along gender lines. This split became most pronounced when the school began to plan their move to a new facility. Although the faculty had input into the architectural plans, the final decision to construct the school with three wings was made by the principal, Renee Black. In keeping with the new structure of the school, she asked the teachers at Explorer Middle School to self-organize into the three houses according to teaching philosophy. Each team was to identify a team philosophy or a theme and give themselves names.

The teachers self-organized into three houses: The 'Power House' and the 'Ropes House', which were comprised entirely of women teachers, and the 'Wolf House', which was comprised of all the men teachers in the school and two women teachers (who were on sabbatical leave when the team and its philosophy were formed). At least on the surface, the houses at Explorer seemed to break down along strict gender lines.

The formations of the Power House and the Ropes House were rather different from the Wolf House. According to a male teacher, prior to the faculty meeting, the women teachers had 'previously aligned themselves . . . [as] . . . a nucleus . . . around a common philosophy of education'. The women teachers in the Power House reinforced this belief, stating: 'I think we were more aggressive in forming our team the way we wanted it to be, and other people sort of sat back and waited for the chips to fall'. In fact, the women teachers in the Power House recruited other women teachers whom they had worked with before from a nearby middle school. The Ropes House also began organizing before the faculty meeting, although they were not quite as established as the Power House.

Unlike the two all-women houses, the Wolf House organized at the last minute without much pre-planning. A teacher in the Wolf House, Bill Jansen, discussed how the Wolf House evolved:

> When the idea was brought up, we were all in the faculty room and the principal asked us to group ourselves with people we thought we could work with as a house . . . So as a joke, I wrote a little note and I passed it along to the other guys saying, 'when we break up, let's have all the guys go stand together, just as a joke'. So when we broke up, all the guys went over and stood in one corner . . . And so it was done purely for humor, but then we realized that there are so few men in this building compared to a usual middle school, and the men started talking and decided it was possible to cover all of the academic areas and actually have a house of just men.

Other male teachers put a less positive spin on the decision. As Mr Carter explained: 'The men gravitated together because the women didn't invite [us]. That's why'. He added that the men teachers at the school felt isolated in this female-dominated school. The gender imbalance in the faculty (i.e., the large majority of teachers were women) was viewed by the male teachers as a product of the principal's hiring preferences. A male teacher stated: 'I don't feel threatened [by the female dominance], but that's the truth [about hiring]'. Another male teacher in the Wolf House stated that in fact the men teachers did feel marginalized by the woman principal and the women teachers: 'If you're in the minority, your way of dealing with things simply never gets addressed'. Similarly, teacher Jim Danson explained that he did not feel as though he received as much affirmation by Ms Black as some women teachers might: 'I coach wrestling and cross country and put on tournaments . . . and [that] doesn't really seem to count for much in Ms Black's eyes as . . . Whereas what we [male teachers] call the touchy-feely stuff, like going to camp [with the students], seems to count for a lot'. By unifying to form a male house, the men teachers hoped to have a stronger voice in the school.

The Wolf House represented a unified male force and Wolf House teachers described the house as all male, even though there were two female teachers who were part of the house as well. These women teachers were part of the house because there were not enough men teachers in the entire school to fully staff the one house. A teacher explained: 'If there were guys out there . . . we might have tried to solicit their membership, but that wasn't the case'. However, in retrospect, he added, 'It's probably better that we have at least one or two [women] on our team just from the standpoint of all the things to do in a given day in a junior high. I mean, you want to have at least one woman on there if nothing else to go into a women's john and check out somebody'. Clearly, the women on the team were not seen as major assets as teaching colleagues.

The name 'Wolf House' evolved from the desire to name the houses for Native clans, which are often identified by animal names. A teacher explained: 'I thought it would be nice for kids to identify with the animals, and we were going to have a mascot of course . . . So we just picked Wolf as kind of a working title'. In contrast, the two women's houses decided not to go with the animal theme. Instead, one group chose to call themselves the 'Power House' because, as they described it, they were teachers who were 'really strong in curriculum and academic success' and were 'all workaholics'. The other women's house called themselves the 'Ropes House', in accordance with the 'Ropes' (Rites of Passage) curricular model to which they subscribed.

The men teachers argued that while they initially grouped together as a joke or as a move for solidarity, after they began to develop their unifying house philosophy, they realized that they had more in common than just gender. A male teacher explained:

> We started out more along gender lines, but then we realized that . . . we shared similar views. My opinion is that there is a correlation between gender and philosophy in education. Not a strict correlation, but certainly the more we talked, the more we realized that there was indeed a lot of commonality among the men and how they saw education as opposed to the women.

Similarly, another teacher stated: 'The [men] were more than free to go align themselves with one of the other groups . . . I think they stayed because they must have seen something they liked'. In other words, a common ideology towards education uniformly appealed to the male teachers. Summing up the ideology of the male teachers and the theme of the Wolf House, Mr Carter, the counselor in the house, stated: 'Well, it's traditional teaching methods . . . The men are going to be labeled "traditional", [although] that's not a cool educational jargon word nowadays. A lot of parents like it, and it just happens to be a basic core value for this group of teachers'. Another teacher in the Wolf House, Bill Jones, explained: 'A good deal of instruction will be done in a manner that most people would recognize as similar to what they had when they went to school'. He added: 'One of our stresses is behavior'. Mr Carter further defined 'traditional' as students working on 'paper/pencil' and some 'drill and response'. He added: 'What we, the guys, see as traditional is building skills and traditional delivery'.

Like the men in the Wolf House who had a strong sense of ideological consensus and solidarity, the women in the Power House described themselves as having strong common beliefs in their unifying theme of progressive teaching methods, such as interdisciplinary units, team teaching, and authentic assessment. The women in the Ropes House had also grouped together around a common progressive theme, the Rites of Passages (ROPES) curricular model, which includes individual education plans for each student and integrated classrooms focused on experiential learning. In the Ropes house, students completed self-directed projects which were evaluated by a group of three community adjudicators. This progressive model, developed at a university, had initially been proposed to the entire faculty by Renee Black.

Both sets of women teachers saw themselves as forming their houses on the basis of common ideologies about education, not on gender grounds. As teacher Brenda Dawes stated, unlike the Wolf House, the Power House teachers 'spent a lot of time thinking about what we wanted and who we wanted to work with'. Similarly, another teacher stated: 'We have lots of cooperation. I think our teams function really well'. The women in the Power House explained that their collaboration went beyond working together for interdisciplinary instruction, for which they were very flexible about scheduling, allowing each other to have longer instructional blocks when necessary. In discussing what made their collaborative efforts work well, a teacher stated: 'We give and take as people rather than resent each other'. This statement appears to be significant as an attempt by these teachers to privilege 'women's ways'.

Gender politics at Explorer seemed to be a two-way street. Men made sexist comments about the women, and women made sexist comments about the men. For example, men in the Wolf House derogatively referred to the Ropes House as the 'In House', because they perceived them to be 'in' with the principal, having chosen her suggested curricular model. Similarly, the women teachers referred to the Wolf House derogatively as the 'Boys' House'. When referring to the 'Wolf House', teacher Brenda Dawes simply commented, 'what a name!'. The women in the Power House joked that if the men's house was the Wolf house, the women's houses could be aptly named the 'Straw House' and the 'Paper House' (referring to *The Three Little Pigs*).

The primacy of gender in the politics of reform in this school also revealed itself in a group interview with seventh grade teachers, where men and women teachers from all three houses were present. The teachers attended a workshop focusing on communication styles in which the speaker had drawn a picture of an iceberg on the board to represent communication. He argued that 90 per cent of the iceberg is beneath the water, representing the fact that 90 per cent of the meaning of speech is actually unspoken. The women teachers explained that they saw clear applications of the iceberg model to gender differences in communication style. Addressing teacher Jim Danson, teacher Paula Simmons remarked: 'We as women look more towards non-verbal things. We listen to you, but we hear the undertones'. Ms Simmons explained, using another male teacher, Tim Walker, as an example: 'If I say "Great job Tim" [said with a sarcastic tone], he hears, "Great job Tim" [tone more upbeat], even though I may have been saying, "God Tim, you *really* screwed up!"'. Anticipating what the men's reaction to Ms Simmons' comment might be, another female teacher remarked: 'Oh God, are we going to pay!'. This discourse, while in jest, is evidence of the salience of gender in this school community and, specifically, the teachers' attention to and perhaps their attempt to rationalize the 'natural' gender differences that might have resulted in their decision to form gender-based houses.

The gender divisions and gender politics among teachers at Explorer Middle School had some damaging effects on the overall school climate and the school's propensity for further reform. For example, teacher John Davis complained that one of the unfortunate outcomes of the gender politics was that all men at the school were stereotyped as being traditional and resistant to reform, even if some (like him) thought of themselves as innovative teachers interested in change. Mr Davis also believed that the structure perpetuated the stereotype of men as subject-oriented and women as interdisciplinary. He found himself in a double bind of not being accepted by the women's houses (because he was male) and not feeling comfortable in the men's house because he did not subscribe to traditional teaching techniques. Yet, he felt he had to ally with his male colleagues, thereby silencing some of his progressive ideas which might have flourished in the other two houses.

According to both men and women teachers, the gender politics at Explorer created a loss of a sense of community. Years after the gender-divided houses were created, the houses remained divided by gender, as did the faculty. Also, based on the men teachers' perception that the principal favored the Ropes House, resentment from the other two houses towards both the principal and that house continued. Women teachers reported that this had resulted in a negative change in the principal's behavior; she evidently became less sympathetic and 'caring' towards teachers than she had been in the past, and more focused on promoting her agenda.

In summary, the story of gender politics at Explorer Middle School was about teachers organizing into theme-based instructional houses on fairly strict gender lines. The men teachers saw this as their only hope to protect their interests in a school dominated by a strong woman principal and the women teachers who represented the majority of the faculty. The women teachers, on the other hand, organized their houses along philosophical lines and in order to have stronger, more collaborative arrangements with each other. The net effect, however, was gender-based houses with distinct ideological differences: The men's house favored traditional teaching techniques and homogeneous grouping and the women's houses favored progressive teaching strategies and heterogeneous grouping.

Before comparing the gender politics at Explorer to the Central High School case, I first turn to a discussion of Grant High School and how gender politics shaped its school change efforts.

Grant High School

A Brief Overview

Serving approximately 1300 students in grades 9 through 12, Grant High School is located in the downtown area of a large city in the western United States. A magnet school for marine sciences and for 'gifted' students, Grant's served a student population which was 50 per cent white, 36 per cent African-American, 9.5 per cent Asian-American, and 5 per cent students of other ethnicities. Grant High School was designated a magnet in the 1970s, under the threat of court ordered desegregation, as this urban school had become increasingly populated by minority students.[3]

Grant was known as one of the finest schools in the district, boasting the largest number of National Merit semi-finalists of any school in the state. However, Grant had a reputation in the community as a 'split' school, academically and racially. It was thought to be an excellent school for students in the honors track who were predominantly white and a mediocre school for students in the general track who were overwhelmingly African-American. The inequities in the school became a matter of serious discussion after the Rodney King trial in 1992. In a school-wide race relations forum following the civil unrest in Los Angeles, the students at Grant identified track-related segregation as one of the major problems at the school. The students challenged the faculty to address the inequities created by tracking in their school.

Accepting the challenge from the students, the English faculty at Grant felt morally compelled to find an alternative to tracking. The department head, Sandi Wright, was very committed to detracking and shared research on tracking and her ideas for reform with other teachers in the department. Moreover, the fact that the English teachers shared a sincere desire to improve their teaching and had strong, collegial relations provided the template for experimentation and innovation in their department.

In a week-long summer planning meeting funded by a special district grant, the English teachers developed their detracking plan. The teachers based their strategy on tracking research, knowledge of other schools' efforts, and on their own discussion about what might work at Grant. The result of the English department's planning was a several-pronged detracking plan, which they instituted in the Fall of 1991. First, they eliminated prerequisites for ninth and tenth grade honors classes, allowing open access to all students; second, they began teaching an identical curriculum to honors and general track sections; third, they rewrote the ninth grade curriculum to focus on world literature, appealing to students' interests; and fourth, they made honors credit an option in all English classes at all grade levels. As a result, many more students elected the honors option, though regular classes still existed on the books.

For a variety of reasons, the other subject departments at Grant did little to respond in a unified way to the students' challenge to end track-related segregation. The history department was highly tracked and had no intention to detrack. The math department was also highly tracked, but offered a summer program for minority students who wished to advance to a higher track. The science department, on the other hand, had no prerequisites for its courses and therefore classes were already mostly heterogeneous.

Gender Politics and Ideological Diversity at Grant High School

The gender divisions at Grant High School, like at Explorer and Central, were rooted in the division between teachers who held traditional and progressive ideologies about education. The teachers who most strongly advocated detracking at Grant were women, and the most vocal detractors tended to be men. Age was not a factor in teachers' support for or opposition to detracking. The progressive camp had its base in the English department, and was most visibly represented by department head Sandi Wright, a twenty-year teaching veteran. There were also many science teachers and teachers from other departments in the progressive camp. The traditional camp had its base in the history department and was most visibly represented by the department chair, Bill Hanford, a seventeen-year teaching veteran who was a former football coach. Teachers in the foreign language and business departments also allied with the traditional camp as well as several teachers from other departments.

The differences in educational ideologies among the traditional and progressive camps at Grant mirrored the divisions at Explorer and Central. Overwhelmingly, the progressive women teachers, including those in the English department, were in favor of detracking and a child-centered approach to education. The traditional men teachers, including those in the history department, were in favor tracking and favored a subject-specialist approach to teaching.

It should be noted that the ideological diversity at Grant, in some ways, had been deliberately planned by Grant's former principal. As the former principal explained:

> When you came as a parent, I could tell you that if you want a real conservative group of teachers, I have that set for you. If you want a group of real strong teachers, but very liberal and easygoing, then I have that group for you.

His strategy was to hire high quality teachers with a variety of teaching styles with less concern about the possibility of personality conflicts among teachers. This resulted in a staff of strong teacher leaders and thus the development of two powerful and rigid camps of teachers, those who were in favor of change and those who were against it, no matter what the issue. In particular, Sandi Wright was noted as a particularly effective leader who inspired her camp of reformers. As one teacher stated: 'She is the kind of person who can make things happen'.

Like the Good Old Boys at Central, the traditional teachers at Grant also took a strong stance against detracking, seeing it as both impractical and irrational. For example, the chair of the history department, Mr Hanford explained his experience fifteen years before with the heterogeneous grouping of regular and college preparatory track students:

> When you start with the higher level explanations, the lower kids can't follow them. They can't keep up with it. They can't associate the dates, the names, and the concepts, and they only get lost. I found that the failure rate of the lower kids soared, even though I gave them modified tests.

He added: 'That's why we went to the tracking system. I've got file cabinets full of lesson plans, assignments, and everything broken down into three levels'. Mr Hanford also justified the track system as being fair to minority students, stating that even when they 'threw the programs open', many African-American students chose not to enroll in advanced classes because of 'peer pressure'.

Like the Good Old Boys at Central, the traditional teachers at Grant saw the problem of low achievement as rooted in the students. Spanish teacher Jim Arnold stated: 'I'm not going to forbear on my children and my wife . . . to re-parent these kids who have been neglected'. Mr Arnold's ideologies about his role as a teacher were rooted in his construction of student ability as related to race. He explained: 'Blacks need the same philosophy that any whites do or Japanese or Chinese. Everybody needs to think correct thoughts. I don't care what color you are'. He added: 'We're not going to change our world to accommodate somebody who doesn't know what to do'. Like the Good Old Boys at Central, the traditional teachers at Grant subscribed to the belief that students who 'buy into' the American dream are more deserving of an education than those who do not. Moreover, in keeping with their views about tracking and student ability, many of the traditional teachers saw students' intelligence as an innate quality that could be accurately measured by standardized test scores (Ray, 1995).

In contrast, teachers in the progressive camp conceived of student ability as having a socially constructed component. Like the Idea Team teachers at Central, the progressive teachers also recognized the existence of multiple types of intelligence (Ray, 1995). For example, in discussing why detracking would be good for all students, a teacher explained that, 'thinking often has nothing to do with skill [level]. Brighter thinkers may be the virgin thinkers. [Although] their skill [level] is low, they've got all these great ideas'. Moreover, she added that unless classes are detracked 'the kid in the higher track is not going to rub elbows with [the low track] kid'.

Accordingly, unlike the history teachers who reported negative experiences with detracking, the English teachers were generally very pleased with the results. Of her experience in teaching the same curriculum to honors and regular track students, a teacher simply stated, '[H]eterogeneity can work!'. Similarly, another teacher who was initially skeptical about whether teaching an honor's curriculum to regular track students would work stated, 'I've turned 180 degrees!'. Although some English teachers conceded that they had not yet managed to bring academic *success* to all students, they agreed that the more challenging curriculum brought benefits for even those students who might not graduate from high school.

In keeping with their common willingness to experiment with detracking innovations, the progressive teachers also shared ideologies about their role as teachers, which is embodied in this statement by English department chair Sandi Wright:

> I connect most with [the teachers] who really sense that we can't afford to waste anybody. We just can't afford to say that we have this [high achieving] group of kids who will carry us . . . they'll be our leaders. I'm convinced we don't live in a world like that anymore. We can't afford to lose those [lower-achieving] kids.

There is an obvious parallel between Ms Wright's comment and the comments of the Idea Team teachers at Central: both sets of teachers felt their mission as teachers was to help all students excel.

Given their divergent beliefs about schooling in general and detracking in particular, it is not surprising that the advent of detracking at Grant High School brought out tensions among the progressive and traditional camps, who had formerly respectfully coexisted. The camps became antagonistic, blaming each other for problems at the school. The progressive camp characterized the traditional camp as 'gatekeepers' who attempted to sabotage change. Progressive teachers also characterized the history teachers as 'fossils', adding that 'they're nice people, but they're already petrified into their positions'.

In turn, the traditional camp characterized the progressive camp as 'unprofessional' teachers who were interested in sacrificing gifted students for foolhardy social goals. The traditional camp also viewed the progressive teachers' efforts as manipulative and political. Discussing this group, a traditional teacher stated: 'There is some real dirty stuff going on in this building. People are trying to do what they want at the expense of others; [they] would actually harm other people's careers and their reputations to get what they want'. This is reminiscent of tactics used by the Good Old Boys at Central to attribute negative career intentions to the reformers.

English department chair Sandi Wright, employing a sexist discourse, commonly referred to Mr Hanford, the history department chair, and his close allies as the 'Testosterone Trio' or the 'troika'. In a further gendered remark about the history department, Ms Wright stated that honors classes in the department were distributed by Mr Hanford to teachers on the basis of 'whether or not they have a penis'. Ms Wright referred to these chosen teachers as Hanford's 'little buddies', and other teachers in the school commonly referred to this small but powerful group of male teachers as the 'Good Old Boys', using the same moniker as at Central.

Conversely, a traditional camp teacher Jim Arnold made offhanded remarks about Ms Wright and her relationship with her 'boyfriend', another teacher in the school. Bill Hanford, indicting Sandi Wright, asserted that the unpopular decisions coming out of the English department, including detracking, resulted from Ms Wright's 'tyranny of the committee'. As he put it, '[if] you don't participate in the committee, you don't have a right to say anything'. Not surprisingly, an English teacher remarked that much of the disapproval Sandi Wright received was due to 'sexism'.[4]

The conflict among the traditional and progressive camps escalated to the point where some members of the English and history departments no longer spoke to each other, a situation which became widely known in the school community among teachers, students, and parents. As Mr Hanford explained, the parents of the gifted students were 'very disturbed about the divisions on the staff'. He described the tension in the school as being 'like Bosnia, with people not talking to each other, and absolutely no leadership'. Another teacher said that the micropolitical conflict among the staff reminded him of the Bolshevik Revolution. He explained: 'Even though they were all communists, they started shooting each other in the back . . . instead of playing out front'. Sandi Wright confirmed this: 'Last year at least we were talking . . . we're now at a point where [Bill Hanford] doesn't even speak to me at all. He doesn't even look at me in the hall'.

In discussing the general climate in the school, a teacher pointed to the 'lack of professional protocol' in the building which allowed some people undue power while silencing the voices of others. Teachers from both the traditional and progressive camps acknowledged Grant High School's climate of tension and frustration. As one teacher summarized, 'the whole school is politicized on virtually every issue you could possibly imagine'. Another teacher remarked that there were 'back stabbers' in the building who used 'dirty pool' to conduct their business.

Not surprisingly, the gender politics at Grant impeded the detracking efforts of the English department. The English teachers suspected that Mr Hanford had spread rumors among parents of the gifted students that they were planning to abolish all honors classes, instead of the actual plan to integrate the honors curriculum into all its classes. Hanford defended himself, stating that talking to parents was 'his only recourse' because the parents 'had the power to do things at the school'.

As a result of this misinformation, the English department focused much of its efforts on damage control instead of moving the detracking movement forward, both within their department and school-wide. The teachers in the English department felt very threatened by the parents of the gifted students, believing that this constituency had considerable power in the district. As one teacher explained: '[The parents] scare the administrators the same way they scare us. They're the last vestiges of the middle class people in the public schools . . . and they scare people with that'. It turns out the English teachers had reason to be concerned: Responding to parent concerns, the principal rejected the department's proposal to eliminate a separate ninth grade honors English class, offering instead an honors option for students in the regular class.

As at Central, the battle for reform between the progressive camp (rooted in the English department) and the traditional camp (rooted in the history department) was fought on the grounds of gender politics. At Grant, gender politics had the net result of slowing down detracking due to the efforts of the male teachers in the history department. Moreover, the gender politics that ensued over reform greatly soured relations among some men and women teachers at the school and resulted in a divisive, antagonistic school culture.

Comparisons to Central High School

Along several dimensions, the gender politics at Explorer and Grant were strikingly, even hauntingly, similar to that of Central. At all three schools, teachers engaged in denigrating sexist discourse as the terrain on which to grapple with differences in power and ideology (which overlapped with gender) during the implementation of detracking reforms. Moreover, at all three schools, detracking was a central feature of the reform, a dimension along which progressive (women) and traditional (men) teachers were sharply divided.

However, based on school culture, the players involved, and the particular reform efforts, the specifics of gender politics at each school differed. Specifically, the three schools varied along the dimensions of who perceived themselves to be the marginalized group in the school and whether the gender factions employed outside constituencies or members of the administration to support their cause. Each of these dimensions, and several others, are discussed in detail below.

Power as Motivating Force

The opportunity for teachers to gain or lose power is an underestimated yet threatening byproduct of whole school reform efforts, particularly those that address existing organizational arrangements. In all three schools, gender politics partly grew out of one group's interest in gaining or maintaining power. At Central and Grant, the traditional male teachers engaged in gender politics in order to preserve their powerful status in the school, and the women teachers stood to gain power if their innovative plans were implemented school-wide. At Explorer, the men teachers sought to gain power and solidarity through their formation of an all-male house. Power is a strong motivating force for both reformist or resistant teacher agency in reform. That is, teacher self-interest is often a subtext to struggles for reform that are couched as being in the interests of students (Ball, 1987).

The Use of Sexist Remarks

In all three schools, the use of sexist remarks and derogatory gender-specific monikers were commonly used by both male and female groups as defensive strategies for their positions on reform. In the accounts of reform, we heard of the 'Testosterone Trio', the 'Good Old Boys', the 'In House', and the 'Dreamers', to name just a few. Moreover, teachers criticized each other's behaviors along gender lines: Women teachers were attacked by men for their decisions to take time off for childbearing, for their personal relationships, and for their supposed ability to rely on their husbands' income. Women at Central even experienced more blatant forms of sexual harassment. Alternately, men teachers were attacked by women for their macho and loud behavior in the faculty room, for their immaturity, and for discriminating against women. Men and women also criticized each other's motivations and philosophies, frequently by attributing a gender base to these actions and ideologies. By and large, women teachers lost out in such discursive battles, and at Central and Grant, they lost out in their plans for reform.

Overlaps in Ideology and Gender

Common to all three schools was the striking overlap of teacher ideology and gender. The men teachers characterized themselves as more traditional, subject matter specialists who favored tracking and thus fought detracking and, in some cases, the 'touchy-feely' reforms that accompanied it. On the other hand, the women teachers characterized themselves as progressive educators who were interested in making schools more nurturing environments where students were provided with a challenging course of study in the context of detracking. That these forceful overlaps in ideology and gender existed at each school points to the need to conduct further inquiry into the ways in which gender socialization and gender relations of power impact the ideologies of men and women secondary teachers. Clearly, there is something here worth investigating.

Changes bring Gender Politics to a Head

In all three schools, proposed change, or the threat of change, brought gender politics among the faculty to the foreground: at Explorer, it was the principal's initiative to group teachers into instructional houses; at Grant, it was the removal of separate honors courses in English (and the perceived threat of this school-wide); and, at Central, it was the implementation of a whole school restructuring plan which included detracking. While ideological and gender differences might have existed in the schools before change entered the picture, it was only when there was a threat to the status quo that gender factionalism and infighting developed among the teachers. It is not surprising, though troubling for the future of school change, that teachers coalesced on gender grounds in the face of reform.

The Connection between Detracking and Gender Politics

Although it was not the specific proposal of detracking that instigated gender politics at Explorer, detracking was a feature of the school's innovative structure, and it was a subject on which traditional (men) and progressive (women) teachers had markedly differing opinions. Detracking was also a centerpiece of the change efforts of teachers at Central and Grant. The political and divisive nature of this reform cannot be understated in those school settings. The defense of the status quo on the part of entrenched male teachers at Central and Grant was a defense of the hierarchy in which both they and white students in the high track were privileged. Arguably, these male teachers' efforts at maintaining the hierarchy of men over women teachers in the school can be seen as part and parcel of their larger movement to maintain tracking's status hierarchy among students.

Gender and Marginalization

Unlike at Central where the women teachers had long been the subjugated group in the school and at Grant where the women teachers struggled against the powerful status quo, it was the men teachers at Explorer Middle School who felt marginalized. At Explorer, the principal's suggestion for teachers to self-organize into houses provided an opportunity for the men teachers in the school to obtain some solidarity and power. While the teachers' formation of a majority-male house was not appreciably threatening to the power of the woman principal or the women teachers, it did serve the function of getting them noticed by the women teachers and, in turn brought gender divisions and gender politics among the faculty to a head. Some of the differences among the schools may have been due to sheer numbers. At Explorer Middle School, where women constituted the great majority of the faculty, the men felt marginalized; clearly, being in a society where men are dominant, it was hard for these teachers to adjust to an arena in which they did not rule the roost. However, in the two high schools, even though there were an equal number of male and female teachers, reflecting societal relations of power, the women teachers constituted the marginalized group.

Departmental Overlaps

At Central and Explorer, the traditional (male) and progressive (female) camps had their roots in a variety of subject disciplines. At Explorer, this was not surprising, as teachers were not departmentalized to begin with, and thus instead the camps had their bases in different 'houses'. By contrast, at Grant, while there were representatives of both camps in various departments, the two camps did have their base in two departments — English (progressive) and history (traditional) — in part because of the strong and contrasting philosophies of the female and male department chairs representing each camp.

Utilizing Outside Constituencies to Bolster Power

At Central and Grant, the traditional male teachers fighting to maintain the status quo (the Good Old Boys and the Testosterone Trio), effectively used their connections to a strong constituency of upper middle class parents as a political strategy. Both the history department chair at Grant and the swim coach at Central (who fought against the custom calendar) were deliberate and open about their efforts to engage and infuriate parents whom they knew would be effective in lobbying against reform at the district level. In contrast, the men in the Wolf House at

Explorer did not engage the support of powerful parents for their cause. However, they felt that their traditional approach to education would be strongly supported by parents who were interested in an educational program that was 'similar to what they had when they were in school'. While it is not surprising that these male teachers, by virtue of their social location as men and their traditional ideologies, were efficacious in pushing their agendas outside the school, these examples point to a formidable barrier in school change.

Administrative Support

Although administrative support was a key variable in the gender politics of educational change at each school, its function varied in interesting ways depending on the role of gender in each school context. At Central and Explorer, the factions of progressive (women) teachers had strong alliances with site administration. This helped them advance their cause, particularly in the case of the Explorer women teachers who received strong support from their female principal and thus little real threat to 'their way of doing things' from the male teachers, although they seemed to feel a loss of political power once the men were a unified group. The Central teachers who were pro-reform also had the backing of their (male) principal, but in this school context even he was not strong enough to withstand the powerful pressure of the Good Old Boys who, it turned out, had a far more powerful reach than he did. Unlike the teachers at Central and Explorer, the predominantly female, progressive English department at Grant did not have the unwavering support of their principal, particularly when he came under fire from parents of gifted students. This absence of support constituted a significant barrier for the reformers, as their nemesis was a group of men teachers who had strong community backing. In essence, it appears that the role of the administrator in the gender politics of reform has a strong contextual basis, depending on the sheer power of patriarchy in a given school and community.

Conclusion: The Effects of Gender Politics in Reform

As the stories of reform at Explorer and Grant suggest, gender politics in educational change is not unique to Central High School. In struggles for power, teachers at each school organized into factions according to their social locations as men and women. The retreat into gender-based factions allowed the battleground of reform to be fought on the terrain of gender as well as, or, in some cases, instead of, ideological diversity regarding education. The shifting of the discourse from education to gender functioned as a political strategy in protecting (generally) male teachers' vested interests.

Although gender political strategies were common to all three schools, what differed was the net effect of gender politics in the ultimate fate of reform. In spite of the loss of community among the teachers at Explorer and the setbacks faced by English teachers at Grant in their move to detrack, unlike what occurred at Central, gender politics did not completely bring down reform at Explorer and Grant. At Central, the Good Old Boys were so politically effective both in and outside the school that few vestiges of reform remain today. At Explorer, however teachers were still organized into houses and students were still hetero-geneously grouped in this innovative middle school. At Grant, change efforts were slowed and teachers encountered significant barriers to reform, but change continued slowly. These varied outcomes of gender politics can be accounted for in the differences in community context, past history of reform, leadership, past histories of patriarchy, and in the sheer power of the gender-based factions at Central compared to Explorer and Grant.

Notes

1   The term 'Native' is used by people at Explorer to refer to American Indian/ Alaska Native students, and as such this abbreviated form is also used in this book.
2   This section on Explorer Middle School draws from the case report on the school (Hirshberg, 1995) and from conversations with its author, Diane Hirshberg.
3   This section on Grant High School draws from the case report on the school (Ray, 1995) and from conversations with its author, Karen Ray.
4   Despite the divisiveness among the two camps, relations *within* departments were generally much more collegial. The math, science, and English depart-ments had very positive within-department relationships, with teachers in each department frequently collaborating. The history department was less cohesive, as it included the core group of men commonly characterized as 'Good Old Boys', as well as at least one male teacher and three female teachers who generally avoided confrontation with this core group of male teachers.

6 Implications for School Change

As the history of reform at the three schools amply illustrates, implementing school change can be tricky business. At Central, the Idea Team's best intentions for reform ran amok in the complex and rocky terrain of gender politics. In many ways, one can look at Central and become depressed about the possibility of reform (or lack thereof) in schools and communities where powerful groups have a strong stake in the status quo. However, on a more optimistic note, several important lessons can be learned from the seedy organizational underworld of school change. Reflecting upon the day-to-day struggles of educators grappling with reform, I conclude this book with some guiding principles for school change.

This conclusion is organized around three major sections: The first section addresses what we have learned about the important role of gender in school change, about the nature of teacher agency in reform, and about the powerful element of micropolitics in school change. The second section addresses specific lessons about school change which can be gleaned from this book. Lastly, I discuss the implications of my findings for further research.

What Have We Learned?

The Important Role of Gender in School Change

As the title of my book suggests, I am very concerned about the powerful role of gender in impacting educational change. Gender operates on the societal level and at the school level as a system of power relations. As the literature on gender and teaching abundantly shows, like other work settings, schools are shaped by social relations of gender in which men are commonly accorded higher status than women. Even in secondary schools, where often at least half of the faculty is female, males still carry the power and authority in schools — and not just at the administrative level, as was once thought.

Since gender is one of the most powerful social organizing features of the lives of teachers in schools, it is not surprising that gender plays such a significant role in school change. Yet, in the past, we have known little about this issue. From this book, we have learned that gender relations among teachers impact reform in two major ways: First, school reform can create or enhance divisiveness among men and women teachers, leading them to retreat into gender-based factions for the purposes of solidarity and power. Moreover, a reform movement led by women teachers is often challenged by men teachers, especially when the reform calls for wholesale deconstruction of the prevailing hierarchies, thereby threatening those teachers, parents, and community leaders who benefit from the old way of doing things.

Second, when teachers retreat into gender-based camps, more often than not the battle over reform is fought on the terrain of gender politics, often employing a sexist discourse, rather than on the terrain of educational issues using an ideological discourse. Why is this? An analysis of the three schools in my book suggests that men teachers who are resistant to change, consciously or not, can shift the focus from reform to gender, where unequal relations of power are pre-organized, in order to more easily prevail over women teachers (and their ideas for reform). This shift in discourse and the entrenchment of teachers into gender-based camps can mean the demise of school reform. While Central High School was no doubt a hotbed of gender politics, the analyses of Explorer and Grant demonstrate that the incidence of gender politics in the school change process is not unique to Central and occurs in schools with vastly different cultures and contexts.

The above lessons about gender dynamics among teachers in reform are especially critical to many current secondary school reforms, especially those that call for altering school structures and cultures to make schools more caring and supportive places for students. The findings of this book suggest that men teachers may be less likely to embrace reforms that ask them to extend their role from subject specialist to nurturing caretaker of students. The men described in this study, at both Central and Explorer, resisted reform efforts which they perceived as asking for 'schools to replace the home'. Men teachers effectively said they would not do 'women's work'. At Central, the Idea Team's total lack of regard for this male conception of reform was probably fatal. Perhaps, the Idea Team should have made greater efforts to couch reform in less gendered ways. On the other hand, realistically, this would have been difficult, as many of the reformers were women and suggested ideas that were rooted in their own experiences. Moreover, because reformers were mostly women, many men teachers at these schools automatically labeled the reforms with gendered attributes.

The Complex Nature of Teacher Agency in School Change

As the above discussion illustrates, undoubtedly teacher agency in school reform is more complex and diverse than many school change theorists and policy makers previously realized, especially when change adopts such a strong political complexion. Teachers who push change are often motivated by progressive ideals for reform, but also for their own personal and professional interests as well. School reforms, if implemented, can make these teachers' work lives more interesting, and by potentially altering existing hierarchies, can result in their gaining more power within the school. However, reform-minded teacher agency has its limitations, as it co-exists with teacher agency aimed at resisting change or, rather, at preserving traditional ideologies and the prevailing structure. In effect, this book has illuminated teacher resistance by exposing some of the strategies entrenched teachers use in the defense of the status quo and how difficult this makes change for the reformers.

By revealing that teacher resistance to change can be both gendered and reactionary, the findings presented in this book are in contrast to arguments that teacher resistance to change is based on age, or career stage, (Huberman, 1989), on sensible political insight against top-down reform (Gitlin and Margonis, 1995), or, more generally, an irrational hostility to change. While resistance to change can have these roots, these are certainly not the only foundations for a rebellion against school change efforts, nor are they consistent with the cases presented in this book. We saw male teachers resistant to change who were roughly the same age (both late in their careers) as the women teachers who were pushing change. We also witnessed resistance to change that was created by teachers internal to the school, rather than the more classic cases of resistance to externally imposed mandates. If we are to more fully understand school change, we need to understand the roots of teacher resistance, how it is expressed in schools, and how teachers in favor of reform respond to such resistance.

Teachers — both for and against reform — are also not unbridled agents in school change. Instead, teacher agency must be understood in terms of its interplay with the structural and cultural features of the school environment and the larger societal structure and culture. Teacher agents with varying ideologies operate within a messy web of cultural politics in the school change process. School change efforts which do not account for the complex nature of teacher agency and the ideological diversity among teachers are likely destined for failure.

However, ideological diversity does not fully explain the different types of teacher agency in reform. My book is not about the productive intellectual debates that occurred among teachers at Central, Explorer, and Grant, assessing various reforms, such as detracking and instructional houses, and determining the best teaching practices or the best strategies for organizing their school. In fact, it is disturbing how seldom students and the educational merits of school change for children were discussed. At Central, the focus on students, and even education in general, got lost in the gender-based power battle between the Good Old Boys and Idea Team. This is the point where micropolitics assumes great importance.

The Powerful Force of Micropolitics in Educational Change

Micropolitics are a powerful force in school change, often becoming *the* focus of reform. Participants in school reform — teachers, administrators, parents, and students — each have their own vested political interests, and, more often than not, these interests are not commonly shared across groups or within groups. In this regard, school reform can be more than just a struggle over the distribution of power and privilege where students are concerned, but also where teachers are concerned. In the case of detracking reforms, this is not so surprising as often teachers engage in an inquiry process around the notion of equity when undertaking such a reform. In the course of such a discussion, a subjugated group of teachers may become enlightened about their own oppression within the school. Thus, the defense of the status quo on the part of entrenched teachers is often a defense of the hierarchy in which both they and, most often, white students in high track classes are privileged. At Central, the Good Old Boys' efforts at maintaining the hierarchy of male over women teachers in the school was part and parcel of their larger movement to maintain tracking's status hierarchy among students.

The connection between language and power in the micropolitics of school reform cannot be underestimated, both in shaping the outcome of a school change effort and in impacting social relations of power. At Central, the voice of the Good Old Boys was literally more loudly heard by community members and administrators than the voice of women on the Idea Team. More powerful groups use language to define what is important in school reform, rendering the definitions of others less important. In this way, powerful groups socially construct the reality of a particular setting. For example, the Good Old Boys at Central and the history department chair at Grant used language to redefine what detracking actually meant in the school by constituting it as something harmful to gifted students. Clearly, language is constitutive of political phenomena and must be recognized as such.

Where Do We Go from Here?

From this knowledge of the complexities of the gender politics of educational change, I have gleaned several lessons for those involved in the process of school change, either as educators or as onlookers.

Policy Makers Cannot Assume that there is Consensus among Teachers over the Goals for Schooling, Much Less the Goals for Reform

How teachers make meaning of the schooling process and their role as teachers varies greatly. This variation affects the ways in which teachers act as agents in reform. All too often, reform in education is about implementing universal change strategies or expanding a program that worked for teachers in one school to other schools. As change theories and packaged school restructuring programs proliferate, there is often little regard to the issue of consensus among the faculty over the goals for reform. Quite simply, each school is a site of ideological differences among teachers. Certainly no set of programs *or* set of change strategies can work for all schools.

Successful Change Requires Addressing Relations of Power between Teachers

An analysis of the three schools presented here suggests that school restructuring must involve significantly redistributing relations of power *among* teachers as well as between teachers and other players in the school. While equitably distributing resources and course load among teachers can help in some schools, differential relations of power often have more to do with the larger structure and culture of which teachers are a part, and therefore flattening the power structure is not so simple. Teachers are part of a society where a power hierarchy exists and the school is one of the meso level institutions in which we can see power relations played out. Therefore, the power hierarchy existing among teachers must be taken into account when planning for or implementing school change.

Part of changing power relations among teachers means paying attention to the discourse that teachers employ in schools. Clearly, in some schools, efforts need to be made to raise the level of civility of everyday discourse, even before reform can be considered. After all, how can we possibility expect to have students embrace equity and treat each other respectfully when the adults in schools are unsuitable role models? The socially constructed nature of relations of power suggests that there is the potential for change when educators question how their own daily behavior contributes to the level of civil discourse and social relations of power in their schools. Discourse in schools is infinitely more productive when the focus is on the children, rather than on adult agendas.

Be Wary of Creating an 'Innovative Elite'

In their recent book on educating adolescents, Hargreaves et al. (1996) discuss the presence in some schools of an 'innovative elite' which cause other teachers to feel excluded from reform efforts. Similarly, this issue of teacher resistance to reforms locally developed by other teachers in their school was present in the case of Central, where the Good Old Boys resisted the locally-developed reform efforts of the Idea Team. Part of changing power relations among teachers involves addressing the question of how a school change effort could be organized so that bottom-up reform stops looking like top-down reform to a sector of the teaching staff. As prior research on school change correctly argues, all teachers need to be involved in the change process if they are to see it as their own, but ideas must germinate somewhere and this often happens among a small group of like-minded teachers. In the end, the architects of reform must ardently consider how the fervor for reform can be generated among the staff and supported by the administration without evolving resistance to an innovative elite.

Reformers Need to Strike a Healthy Balance between Idealism and Pragmatism

As factions fighting a micropolitical battle, neither the Idea Team nor the Good Old Boys gave much thought to compromise on the infighting or the extent to which reforms could realistically be implemented in their school. This was probably not surprising, as the Central school culture was characterized by a long history of animosity between men and women teachers. While keeping an eye on their ideals, reformers also need to pay more attention to issues of 'realpolitiks' in their school. Clearly, this did not happen at Central. In fact, the reformers, the Idea Team, were often derogatively referred to as the 'Dream Team' by the Good Old Boys and school board president Bill Bathgate, partly for their strong attention to ideals and weaker attention to practicalities. By associating the Idea Team as the 'Dream Team' rather than as colleagues with some compelling, implementable ideas, the Good Old Boys defined reform at Central as unworkable and misguided. The Good Old Boys viewed the reform efforts as practical disruptions either to their school schedules, vacations, or pedagogic practices. Yet, the Idea Team and principal Bob Foster never considered working reform around the complaints of the Good Old Boys.

In the end, we are left wondering whether reform would have been more successful at Central if the Idea Team and the principal Bob Foster had been more pragmatic in terms of dealing with the Good Old Boys, perhaps by meeting some of their needs while also remaining true to the ideals of reform. In the case of Central, arguably, the Idea Team might not have been willing to compromise at all; and, similarly, the Good Old Boys might simply have refused incorporating almost any type of reform. Either way, for reformers, striking a balance between idealism and pragmatism, especially in a hostile school environment, requires rather deft political skills.

Know When to Choose an Incremental versus a Radical School Change Strategy

A corollary to the issue of idealism versus pragmatism is knowing when to choose to implement school change incrementally or radically. Bogged down in a gender political battle with the Good Old Boys, the Idea Team did not capitalize on their success in implementing less sweeping reforms on the departmental level, when in fact it was significant that several Idea Team members were able to gain consensus for at least some curricular changes in individual departments. Possibly, the Idea Team teachers should have concentrated on incremental reform, particularly in the contested political terrain of Central High School.

Proponents of incrementalism argue that it is the best way to bring about change while maintaining stability and consensus. There are of course downsides to an incremental approach to change. Change is slower when incrementally implemented. Additionally, as Hochschild

(1984) argues that in the case of school desegregation, 'to make a few changes in education and wait for them to produce good results before undertaking more is exactly the wrong strategy', producing either insufficient changes or worse yet, the wrong changes (p. 86). However, when considered in terms of Gramsci's (1971) model for social change, incrementalism in the realm of whole school change has greater possibilities. Gramsci suggests strategies for change in environments where ideology is contested, wherein agents function as 'organic intellectuals' within different subcultures to promote critical consciousness among the entire staff and among the community. The lack of critical consciousness regarding current schooling practices among the whole faculty, especially the majority teachers who constituted the Middle Group, contributed to the downfall of reform at Central. At Central a strategy of incremental change at least had the potential, even if realistically slim, of bringing the key swing block of teachers, the Middle Group, on to the reform bandwagon.

Implications for Further Research

My hope is that this book will pave the way for future studies on the nexus of gender, school reform, and micropolitics. More generally, in future studies of school change, we need to open wider the black box of the school reform process by asking the following questions: 1) Whose interests are being served by the current system? 2) Whose interests would be served by the proposed change? 3) How are school cultures contested and negotiated, and by whom? 4) Finally, how are professional relationships between teachers influenced by class, race, and gender relations, and how might these relationships be impacted by reform?

Keeping these broad questions in mind, the micropolitics of reform ought to be acknowledged and studied, as it is often the key factor in the success or failure of change efforts. We can no longer afford to view micropolitics as a pariah in school change research. In particular, we ought to conduct studies of micropolitics in the context of current school reform policies which propose dramatic changes to schools, as this is where the micropolitics of school reform are most evident. For example, while policymakers urge sweeping reforms which rely on teachers to 'reinvent' schools, as this book illustrates, in reality, this is not so easy in many schools. As educators and researchers, we need to learn more about how teachers with competing interests and ideologies gain consensus on the means and the substance of school change.

Although gender was the micropolitical terrain of reform in the three schools discussed in this book, the terrain of micropolitics truly varies according to the particular characteristics of the players, the school context, and the wider social and political context. In other words, we need to focus on the other principles of social differentiation that can impact reform, such as race, social class, or ethnicity. For example, in a school or community with potential for racial divisions, race could fill the role of gender as the salient issue around which the micropolitics of reform are organized. In fact, a colleague of mine recently recounted a 'race riot' that ensued among teachers in a school which was attempting reform. At this school, racial tensions had evidently existed beneath the surface but were brought to the foreground when change was proposed. Undoubtedly, there are other schools in which racial differences among teachers become the subject of school reform and the discourse of reform may again shift to one along racial lines. In point of fact, agents in reform retreat to social location, where hierarchies are pre-organized, in defense of their position.

It is not enough to say that politics got in the way of successful reform. Studies of the micropolitics of school change need a theoretical framework for understanding how the politics plays themselves out. We need to know how, why, and whether this might happen elsewhere — a perspective which only a well-grounded theory can provide. We clearly need a multi-disciplinary perspective for studying the complexities school change. In addition, researchers should be aware that collecting data on school micropolitics can be a difficult and delicate business. Because politics have long been a taboo subject in schools, educators might not want to air their dirty laundry to the outside world. Collecting data on such issues requires asking the right questions and, most importantly, building trust with educators through a long-term relationship and assurances that their identities will be held in confidence. By revealing their own experiences in school reform, educators can potentially help their counterparts in other schools avoid political land mines. Researchers also need to be careful not to become embroiled in the middle of school micropolitics; this is a downside of being an outsider privy to insider information.[1]

Naturally, studies of the micropolitics of school change must attend to gender issues. However, the dearth of gender issues in school change research is so striking that the role of gender in and of itself in shaping school change deserves special attention. Women teachers are subject to material and ideological forces related to their gender that may impact both their reform efforts, particularly where equity is concerned, and their professional lives as teachers (Weiler, 1988). We need to know much more about the role of gender in impacting educational change.

In particular, it would be fruitful to examine gender politics in the context of other reform efforts, as this book focused solely on schools undertaking detracking, albeit along with other reforms. Other reforms which also have the potential to alter the status quo substantially, such as systemic reform or site-based decision making, may provide interesting contexts in which to examine gender politics. It would also be interesting to examine gender politics in the context of smaller school change efforts such as 'school within a school' reforms to see how they play out on a more localized level. Moreover, further research is certainly needed into the role gender plays in educational change at the elementary level. Since elementary schools are comprised primarily of women teachers and since fewer elementary school reform models challenge existing power hierarchies among teachers, the gender politics of educational change may take on a different character in an elementary setting. Overall, on a number of levels, further research into the gender politics of educational change is merited. This book is only a first step in that direction.

Conclusion

This book has pointed out the complicated dynamics of what happens when gender politics infiltrates the school change process. In particular, school reform can evoke a struggle between factions of teachers over whose definition of 'school' will prevail, but the focus of this struggle may be not education, but gender. Given these political complexities, transforming our schools into better learning environments for children is not likely to be easy, but that does not mean that we should abandon the goal. After all, often it is in the schools where change is most difficult, where the teachers are most entrenched and the struggle to maintain the status quo is the hardest fought, that reform is most needed and students are at the greatest disadvantage. We must work harder to find strategies for school change that address the political and contested nature of change in schools.

Note

1   See Datnow and Ray, 1994, for a more detailed discussion of this insider-outsider dilemma.

Appendix: Sample Teacher Interview Protocol for the *Beyond Sorting and Stratification Study*[1]

I Background

A. Personal History

1. How long have you been a teacher? How long at this school?
2. Describe your current teaching assignment.

B. Political/Educational Context

1. What is the standing of this school among schools in the community?
2. What is important in this community in terms of education — (Students getting into college? Test scores? Sports teams?)
3. How influential is the teachers' union here?

II Change Strategies

1. Is the school currently involved in reform efforts other than detracking?
    If so, how do they relate to the detracking effort, and is it competing with other reforms for resources or support?
2. What was done to prepare the faculty for detracking?
    Do you feel these efforts were helpful?
    Sufficient? What else could have been or should still be done?
3. Have the purposes and goals of detracking been well communicated to faculty members?
    Is there widespread support among the faculty for the detracking effort?
    Is this support increasing or decreasing?
4. Has there been resistance to the detracking effort?
    If so, what form has the resistance taken?

If not, what, if anything, has been done in response to this resistance?

5. Who was involved in developing the detracking strategy?
   Were the same people who initiated detracking in your school also involved in developing the detracking strategy?
   If not, how were these two groups different?

IF teachers were involved in developing the detracking plan:

6. Is the detracking strategy based on a specific model or approach?
7. What changes have occurred in the detracking strategy since its inception?
8. Are you comfortable with the pace of detracking?
9. Are you comfortable with the extent of the detracking effort? (Would you prefer it to be more comprehensive, for example, more grades, subjects, or departments involved or would you prefer that it was smaller, more like a pilot study?)

III   Organization and Staffing

1. Are meetings held regularly to discuss reforms, events, decisions, etc.?
   Who attends (teachers, students, parents)?
   Who talks at these meetings?
   Are everybody's opinions valued?
   What decisions are made and who makes them?
   What happens when there are conflicts?
   What have you learned at these meetings, if anything?
2. How much choice do you have in your classroom and/or team assignments?
   Is this different since detracking began?
3. Do you feel you have the classroom resources you need to perform your job effectively?
   Is this different since detracking began?
4. How much control do you have over the selection of instructional materials? — complete, some, none?
   Is this different since detracking began?
5. How much control do you have over the planning and writing of curriculum?
   Is this different since detracking began?
6. How much control do you have over planning and spending the budget for your department? for the school in general?
   Is this different since detracking began?

7. How much control do you have over hiring other teachers?
   Is this different since detracking began?
8. If you could change your teaching assignment in any way, how would you change it?

IV School-wide Climate/Ethos

A. School Efficacy

1. Do you think most adults in this school feel responsible when students succeed?
   If so, why do you think they feel this way?
2. Can you give us an example of a student for whom the school really made a difference?
3. Do you think most adults in this school also feel responsible when students are not successful?
4. Characterize the students for whom adults feel responsible?
5. Characterize the students for whom adults don't feel responsible?

B. Individualism and Community

1. Do students have a great deal of school spirit?
   Is this different since detracking began?
2. Do students here tend to compete with each other?
   What about staff?
   Is this different since detracking began?

C. Curriculum/Pedagogy/Assessment — Classroom Regularities

1. Has your approach to curriculum changed since detracking began?
2. Have your methods of teaching changed since detracking began?
3. What about your methods of assessment?
4. How effective are you at teaching?
   Is this different since detracking began?
5. Do you feel differently about the kind of teaching you have provided since detracking began?
6. If you could have the 'ideal' curriculum, what would you like to see?

7. How would you answer that question if all of the students here were white and middle class? (Probe for explanation of why different or same.)
8. How is this ideal different from what you might have said when you first started teaching?
9. What might it take to make your vision of the ideal a reality? What now gets in the way?
10. Do you think the students at this school are 'smart enough' to succeed in the curriculum you think would be 'ideal'?
11. When people use the term 'multicultural education' here, what do they mean? How salient is multicultural education?
12. Are there any requirements that include multicultural curriculum here?
13. Is there anyone here (state, district, or school) who you would consider to be an 'advocate' for multicultural education? Has their advocacy made a difference?
14. How are excellence and equity defined, especially related to classroom practice?
15. Do you do anything in your classroom to raise students' awareness about such issues as racism, sexism, competition and individualism in society, etc.? How do you see this as connected to detracking?

D.   *Teachers' Working Conditions*

1. Are teachers here collegial and cooperative?
   Is this different since detracking began?
2. In what ways do teachers think about the school as a whole?
   Is this different since detracking began?
3. Do you feel able to talk about any grievances or concerns with regard to detracking and its impact on your classroom?

E.   *Administrative Leadership*

1. How would you describe the principal's leadership at this school?
   Is this different since detracking began?

IF other administrator or teacher is leading the detracking effort, ask the these questions about him/her

2. Has the principal been effective in communicating to the faculty the reasons for detracking?

3. Has he/she been effective in addressing concerns or conflicts related to detracking?

F. Social Construction of Race and Ability

1. Are there some students you enjoy teaching more than others? If so, why?
2. How achievement oriented are students at this school? Is there a wide range?
      Is this different since detracking began?
3. In what ways are students identified as smart by faculty? by students?
      Is this different since detracking began?
4. Now, this school has been racially mixed since X (or always).
      Has the faculty employed specific strategies for helping students of different racial/ethnic backgrounds get along?
      Is this different since detracking began?
5. Do you think students of different racial or ethnic groups get along?
      Do students participate in many of the same extracurricular activities?
      Do you think students of different racial/ethnic groups socialize together outside of school?)
      Is this different since detracking began?
6. Do you think that certain groups of students seem to have social or academic power at the school? Is one group better represented in leadership roles in the school? Is this different since detracking began?
7. Do you think that students are characterized by others on the basis of their race or ethnicity? Explain.
      What about the faculty?
      Is this different since detracking began?
8. Is there much racial conflict and hostility at the school?
      What is the nature of this conflict (fighting, name calling, exclusion)?
      Who is the target of much of this conflict?
      Does it come from students, teachers, staff?
9. Do certain ethnic groups maintain their own ethnic identity?
      How does their ethnic identity effect their ability to succeed in the school? To fit in at the school?
10. Is improving race relations a reason for detracking? If not, why not?

11. What attitudes and values about race do you feel must be addressed before a successful detracking program can be implemented?

12. What impact does the racial composition of the student body have on the social and academic climate?

13. Are race and race relations openly talked about among staff and students?
    If so in what way — what forum?
    If not why, why not?
    Is this different since detracking began?

14. Do you consider the cultural diversity at this school when planning your curriculum?
    If yes, in what manner?
    If no, why not?

15. Do you use any techniques to minimize racial segregation within your classroom?
    If so, what are these techniques and how successful are they?

16. Do students of all ethnic groups have the same opportunity to attend college? Are some ethnic groups attending different types of colleges than others? What causes the diversity in college choice (academic preparation, career aspirations, financial?)

V Contact with Community/Parents

1. How frequently do you contact the parents of your students?
   Is this different since detracking began?

2. What usually prompts you to contact a parent?
   Are there times when parents contact you?

3. Who are the more active parents?
   Describe some of the ways parents want to be involved in the education of their children.
   Do parents ever come and sit in on your classroom?

4. Do you see support for detracking from the community and the parents as increasing, decreasing, or staying the same over time? Why?

5. How do parents try to influence decisions or practices at this school? Which parents do which kinds of things?
   Are these efforts by parents seen as reasonable? By everyone?

6. Does faculty or administration ever try to get parents to exert their influence? Who? How? When? Why? With what effect?

7. If you could change the way parents influence things at the school, what would you have them do differently?

VI   Student Power

1. Are students given an opportunity to affect change in their education? How can they do so?
   Does the staff value their input?
2. Are there benefits for all students when/now that detracking is implemented?
   Are these benefits equally distributed among all students no matter what their past placement?
3. Do you think most students support the detracking effort?
4. Was there one ethnic group more vocal in their reactions to detracking?
5. What do you think students think or feel about school?
   Do they reflect their parents' views?
6. Does the school consider student empowerment as one of the markers of a successful education?

VII   About the Implementation of Detracking/Advice for Other Schools

1. I'd like to ask you to imagine that you've been asked by another school (district, state) to give advice about how to go about a reform effort like the one you're involved in here. What have you learned from your experience here that you would want to tell them?
2. What would you suggest in the area of curriculum? Is there a 'bottom line' in this area? That is, would you say, 'Don't even try it unless . . .'? What about teaching strategies? Assessment? Scheduling? What institutional barriers would you warn people about?
3. Does detracking require teachers to think very differently? Specifically, how might their thinking have to change? How does this kind of change happen? How do values have to change in this kind of a reform? What unspoken 'rules' or traditions at the school might be violated by detracking?
4. What might you say to a school about how to smooth the way for these changes with other faculty? (to get at political issues) With parents? With the district office and the Board?
5. What might you say to people about how relationships within a school ought to change if the reform is to be successful? Does this require more sharing of resources? Does it threaten the status system in the school? If so, ask how people who had a lot of status or privilege in the old system (the high track kids, high track

teachers, high track parents) might be helped to feel comfortable with detracking?

6. How does detracking affect the school as a professional community? Is it in teachers' self-interest to pursue detracking? What do teachers have to give up to be part of this reform? What do they gain? Where do teachers draw the line? That is, what wouldn't they give up for this reform?

7. What role does 'research', 'expert knowledge', and school-based inquiry and experimentation (e.g., pilots, collecting data, evalution) play in detracking a school? Is detracking something you're comfortable talking with each other about here? How hard is it to get people to consider these new ideas? What does it take to convince people here to try something new? Is this something that a school can do pretty easily?

8. What is most likely to be responsible if these types of reforms don't succeed at a school? (i.e., who has the power to make things fail?)

9. What do you think this school will be like in five years?

Note

1 This interview protocol was developed specifically for the *Beyond Sorting and Stratification* study by Jeannie Oakes and Army Wells and the eight research associates on this study, including myself.

References

ACKER, S. (Ed.) (1989) *Teachers, Gender, and Careers*, London: Falmer Press.

ACKER, S. (1994) *Gendered Education: Sociological Reflections on Women, Teaching, and Feminism*, Bristol, PA: Open University Press.

ALEXANDER, J. (1987) *Twenty Lectures: Sociological Theory Since World War II*, New York: Columbia University Press.

ANYON, J. (1981) 'Social class and school knowledge', *Curriculum Inquiry*, **11**, pp. 3–41.

APPLE, M.W. (1985) *Education and Power*, Boston: Routledge and Kegan Paul.

APPLE, M.W. (1994) 'Is change always good for teachers? Gender, class, and teaching in history', in BORMAN, K. and GREENMAN, N. (Eds) *Changing American Education: Recapturing the Past or Inventing the Future?*, Albany, NY: SUNY Press.

BAHKTIN, M. (1981) 'Discourse and the novel', in EMERSON, C. and HOLQUIST, M. (Eds) *The Dialogic Imagination*, Austin, TX: University of Texas Press.

BALL, S.J. (1987) *The Micro-Politics of the School: Towards a Theory of School Organization*, New York: Routledge.

BERGER, P. and LUCKMANN, T. (1967) *The Social Construction of Reality*, New York: Doubleday.

BIKLEN, S.K. (1995) *School Work: Gender and the Cultural Construction of Teaching*, New York: Teachers College Press.

BLACKMORE, J. and KENWAY, J. (1995) 'Changing schools, teachers, and curriculum: But what about the girls?', in CORSON, D. (Ed.) *Discourse and Power in Educational Organizations*, Cresskill, NJ: Hampton Press.

BLASE, J. (1989) 'The teachers' political orientation vis-a-vis the principal: The micropolitics of the school', in HANNAWAY, J. and CROWSON, R. (Eds) *The Politics of Reforming School Administration*, Philadelphia: Falmer Press, pp. 113–26.

BLASE, J. (1993) 'The micropolitics of effective school-based leadership: Teachers' perspectives', *Educational Administration Quarterly*, **29**, 2, pp. 142–63.

BRADDOCK, J.H. and DAWKINS, M.P. (1993) 'Ability grouping, aspirations, and attainments: Evidence from the national educational longitudinal study of 1988', *Journal of Negro Education*, **62**, pp. 324–36.

CARNEGIE FOUNDATION FOR THE ADVANCEMENT OF TEACHING (1988) *The Condition of Teaching: A State-by-State Analysis (Technical Report)*, Princeton: Carnegie Foundation for the Advancement of Teaching.

CASEY, K. (1993) *I Answer With my Life: Life Histories of Women Teachers Working for Social Change*, New York: Routledge.

CASEY, K. and APPLE, M.W. (1989) 'Gender and the conditions of teachers' work: The development of understanding in America', in ACKER, S. (Ed.) *Teachers, Gender, and Careers*, London: Falmer Press.

COHEN, E., KEPNER, D. and SWANSON, D. (1995) 'Dismantling status hierarchies in heterogeneous classrooms', in OAKES, J. and QUARTZ, K.H. (Eds) *Creating New Educational Communities*, Chicago, IL: National Society for the Study of Education.

COMMON DESTINY ALLIANCE (1992) 'Realizing our nation's diversity as an opportunity: Alternatives to sorting America's children', (Final Report to the Lilly Endowment, Inc.) Washington DC: Common Destiny Alliance.

CORBETT, H.D. and ROSSMAN, G. (1989) 'Three paths to implementing change', *Curriculum Inquiry*, **19**, 2, pp. 163–90.

CORSON, D. (1995) 'Discursive power in educational organizations: An introduction', in CORSON, D. (Ed.) *Discourse and Power in Educational Organizations*, Cresskill, NJ: Hampton Press.

CRAWFORD, M. (1995) *Talking Difference: On Gender and Language*, London: Sage.

CUBAN, L. (1988) *The Managerial Imperative and the Practice of Leadership in the Schools*, Albany, NY: SUNY Press.

CUNNISON, S. (1989) 'Gender joking in the classroom', in ACKER, S. (Ed.) *Teachers, Gender, and Careers*, London: Falmer Press.

DARLING-HAMMOND, L. (1990) 'Instructional policy into practice: The power of the bottom over the top', *Educational Evaluation and Policy Analysis*, **12**, 3, pp. 233–41.

DATNOW, A. (1995) 'Making sense of teacher agency: Linking theory to school reform policy', unpublished doctoral dissertation, Los Angeles, CA: UCLA.

DATNOW, A. and RAY, K. (1994) 'Exploring our role: Responsibility and sensitivity in case study research', paper presented at the annual meeting of the American Educational Research Association, New Orleans, LA.

DEAL, T.E. and KENNEDY, A. (1983) 'Culture and school performance', *Educational Leadership*, **40**, 5, pp. 140–41.

DREEBEN, R. (1970) *The Nature of Teaching*, Glenview, IL: Scott Foresman.

ELMORE, R. (1996) 'Getting to scale with good educational practice', *Harvard Educational Review*, **66**, 1, pp. 1–26.

FINLEY, M.K. (1984) 'Teachers and tracking in a comprehensive high school', *Sociology of Education*, **57**, pp. 233–43.

FOUCAULT, M. (1984) *The Foucault Reader*, New York: Penguin Books.

FULLAN, M. (1991) *The New Meaning of Educational Change,* New York: Teachers College Press.

FULLAN, M. (1993) *Change Forces: Probing the Depths of Educational Reform*, London: Falmer Press.

FULLAN, M. and HARGREAVES, A. (1996) *What's Worth Fighting for in Your School?*, New York: Teachers College Press.

GARDNER, H. (1983) *Frames of Mind: The Theory of Multiple Intelligences,* New York: Basic Books.

References

GHERARDI, S. (1995) *Gender, Symbolism, and Organizational Cultures*, London: Sage.

GIDDENS, A. (1979) *Central Problems in Social Theory, Action, Structure, and Contradiction in Social Analysis*, London: Macmillan.

GILLIGAN, C. (1982) *In a Different Voice: Psychological Theory and Women's Development,* Cambridge: Harvard University Press.

GIROUX, H. (1984) 'Ideology, agency, and the process of schooling', in BARTON, L. and WALKER, S. (Eds) *Social Crisis and Educational Research*, London: Croom and Helm.

GIROUX, H.A. and MCLAREN, P. (1986) 'Teacher education and the politics for engagement: The case for democratic schooling', *Harvard Educational Review,* **56**, 3, pp. 213–38.

GITLIN, A. and MARGONIS, F. (1995) 'The political aspect of reform: Teacher resistance as good sense', *American Journal of Education*, **103**, pp. 377–405.

GOODSON, I. (1991) 'Sponsoring the teacher's voice', in HARGREAVES, A. and FULLAN, M. (Eds) *Understanding Teacher Development,* New York: Teachers College Press.

GRAMSCI, A. (1971) *Selections From the Prison Notebooks,* New York: International Publishers.

GRANT, R. (1989) 'Women teachers' career pathways: Towards an alternative model of career', in ACKER, S. (Ed.) *Teachers, Gender, and Careers*, London: Falmer Press.

GRAY, J. (1992) *Men are From Mars, Women are From Venus,* New York: Harper Collins.

HARGREAVES, A. (1993) 'Personal impractical knowledge? Teachers' experiences of restructuring', paper presented at the annual meeting of the American Educational Research Association, Atlanta, Georgia.

HARGREAVES, A. (1994) *Changing Teachers, Changing Times*, New York: Teachers College Press.

HARGREAVES, A., EARL, L. and RYAN, J. (1996) *Schooling for Change: Reinventing Education for Early Adolescents*, London: Falmer Press.

HARGREAVES, A. and HOPKINS, D. (1991) *The Empowered School: The Management and Practice of Development Planning,* London: Cassell.

HECKMAN, P. and PETERMAN, F. (1997) 'Indigenous invention and school reform', *Teachers College Record*, **98**, 2, pp. 307–27.

HIRSHBERG, D.B. (1995) *Explorer Middle School Case Report,* Los Angeles: Research for Democratic School Communities, UCLA Graduate School of Education.

HOCHSCHILD, J. (1984) *The New American Dilemma: Liberal Democracy and School Desegregation,* New Haven: Yale University Press.

HOPKINS, D. and WIDEEN, M.F. (1984) *New Perspectives on School Improvement,* London: Falmer Press.

HOYLE, E. (1986) *The Politics of School Management,* London: Hodder and Stoughton.

HUBERMAN, M. (1989) 'The professional life cycle of teachers', Teachers College Record, **91**, 2, pp. 30–57.

HUBERMAN, M. and MILES, M. (1984) *Innovation Up Close: How School Improvement Works,* New York: Plenum.

IANNACCONE, L. (1991) 'Micropolitics of education: What and why', *Education and Urban Society*, **23**, 4, pp. 465–71.

KANPOL, B. (1992) *Toward a Theory and Practice of Teacher Cultural Politics: Continuing the Postmodern Debate*, New Jersey: Ablex Publishing.

KULIK, C.C. and KULIK, J.A. (1982) 'Effects of ability grouping on secondary school students: A meta-analysis of the evaluation findings', *American Education Research Journal*, **19**, pp. 415–28.

LABOV, T. (1990) 'Ideological themes in reports of interracial conflict', in GRIMSHAW, A.D. (Ed.) *Conflict Talk: Sociolinguistic Investigations of Arguments in Conversations,* Cambridge: Cambridge University Press, pp. 139–59.

LAKOFF, G. and JOHNSON, M. (1975) *Metaphors We Live By*, Chicago: University of Chicago Press.

LANDE, C. (1977) 'Introduction: The dyadic basis of clientelism', in SCHMIDT, S., GUASTI, L., LANDE, C. and SCOTT, J.C. (Eds) *Friends, Followers, and Factions,* Berkeley: University of California Press.

LIEBERMAN, A. (Ed.) (1995) *The Work of Restructuring Schools: Building From the Ground Up*, New York: Teachers College Press.

LIPMAN, P. (1997) 'Restructuring in context: A case study of teacher participation and the dynamics of ideology, race, and power', *American Educational Research Journal*, **34**, 1, pp. 3–37.

LORTIE, D.C. (1975) *School Teacher: A Sociological Study*, Chicago: University of Chicago Press.

MALEN, B. (1995) 'The micropolitics of education: mapping multiple dimensions of power relations in school polities', in SCRIBNER, J.D. and LAYTON, D.H. (Eds) *The Study of Educational Politics*, London: Falmer Press.

MALEN, B. and OGAWA, R.T. (1988) 'Professional-patron influence on site-based governance councils: A confounding case study', *Educational Evaluation and Policy Analysis*, **10**, pp. 251–79.

MANGHAM, I. (1979) *The Politics of Organizational Change*, Westport, CN: Greenwood Press.

MANN, P. (1994) *Micro Politics: Agency in a Postfeminist Era*, Minneapolis: University of Minnesota Press.

MARSHALL, C. and SCRIBNER, J. (1991) 'It's all political: Inquiry into the micropolitics of education', *Education and Urban Society*, **23**, 4, pp. 347–55.

McLAUGHLIN, M.W. (1994) 'Strategic sites for teachers' professional development', in GRIMMETT, P. and NEUFELD, J. (Eds) *Teacher Development and the Struggle for Authenticity*, New York: Teachers College Press.

McLAUGHLIN, M.W. and TALBERT, J.E. (1993) 'How the world of students and teachers challenges policy coherence', in FUHRMAN, S.H. (Ed.) *Designing Coherent Educational Policy*, San Francisco: Jossey Bass.

McLaughlin, M.W., Talbert, J.E. and Bascia, N. (Eds) (1990) *The Contexts of Teaching in Secondary Schools: Teachers' Realities*, New York: Teachers College Press.

McNeil, L.M. (1988) *Contradictions of Control: School Structure and School Knowledge*, New York: Routledge.

Mead, G.H. (1934) *Mind, Self, and Society from the Standpoint of a Social Behaviorist*, Chicago: University of Chicago Press.

Mehan, H. (1990) 'Oracular reasoning in a psychiatric exam: the resolution of conflict in language', in Grimshaw, A. (Ed.) *Conflict Talk*, Cambridge: Cambridge University Press.

Mehan, H. (1993) 'Beneath the skin and between the ears: A case study in the politics of representation', in Shaiklin, S. and Lave, J. (Eds) *Understanding Practice: Perspectives on Activity and Context*, Cambridge: Cambridge University Press.

Mehan, H., Nathanson, C. and Skelly, J. (1990) 'Nuclear discourse in the 1980s: The unraveling conventions of the Cold War', *Discourse and Society*, **1**, 2, pp. 133–65.

Metz, M.H. (1978) *Classrooms and Corridors: The Crisis of Authority in Desegregated Secondary Schools*, Berkeley, CA: University of California Press.

Miles, M. and Huberman, M. (1984) *Qualitative Data Analysis*, Beverly Hills, CA: Sage Publications.

Nias, J. (In press) 'Why teachers need their colleagues: A developmental perspective', in Hargreaves, A., Lieberman, A., Fullan, M. and Hopkins, D. (Eds) *International Handbook of Educational Change*, Hingman, MA: Kluwer.

Noblit, G., Berry, B. and Demsey, V. (1991) 'Political responses to reform: A comparative case study', *Education and Urban Society*, **23**, 4, pp. 379–95.

Oakes, J. (1985) *Keeping Track: How Schools Structure Inequality*, New Haven, CT: Yale University Press.

Oakes, J. (1987) 'Tracking in secondary schools: A contextual perspective', *Educational Psychologist*, **22**, 2, pp. 129–53.

Oakes, J. (1990) *Multiplying Inequalities: The Effects of Race, Social Class, and Tracking on Opportunities to Learn Math and Science*, Santa Monica, CA: The Rand Corporation.

Oakes, J., et al. (1993) 'There is life after tracking', *Doubts and Certainties*, **7**, 6, pp. 1–5.

Oakes, J., Gamoran, A. and Page, R. (1992) 'Curriculum differentiation: Opportunities, outcomes, and meanings', in Jackson, P. (Ed.) *Handbook of Research on Curriculum*, New York: Macmillan.

Oakes, J. and Lipton, M. (1992) 'Detracking schools: Early lessons from the field', *Phi Delta Kappan*, **73**, 6, pp. 448–54.

Oakes, J. and Wells, A.S. (1995) 'Beyond sorting and stratification: Creating alternatives to tracking in racially mixed secondary schools', paper presented at the annual meeting of the American Educational Research Association, San Francisco, CA.

OAKES, J. and WELLS, A. (1996) *Beyond the Technicalities of School Reform: Lessons from Detracking Schools*, Los Angeles: Center X, Graduate School of Education and Information Studies, UCLA.

OAKES, J., WELLS, A., DATNOW, A. and JONES, M. (1997) 'Detracking: The social construction of ability, cultural politics, and resistance to reform', *Teachers College Record*, **98**, 3, pp. 482–510.

O'NEIL, J. (June, 1993) 'Can separate be equal? Educators debate merits, pitfalls of tracking', *Curriculum Update*, pp. 7–14.

RAY, K.A. (1995) *Grant High School Case Report*, Los Angeles: Research for Democratic School Communities, UCLA Graduate School of Education.

REGAN, H.B. and BROOKS, G.H. (1995) *Out of Women's Experience: Creating Relational Leadership*, Thousand Oaks, CA: Corwin Press.

RESTINE, N. (1993) *Women in Administration: Facilitators for Change*, Newbury Park, CA: Corwin Press.

RICH, A. (1979) *On Lies, Secrets, and Silence*, New York: Norton.

RIDDELL, S. (1989) ' "It's nothing to do with me": Teachers' views and gender divisions in the curriculum', in ACKER, S. (Ed.) *Teachers, Gender, and Careers*, London: Falmer Press.

SARASON, S. (1990) *The Predictable Failure of Educational Reform*, San Francisco: Jossey Bass.

SARASON, S. (1996) *Revisiting 'The Culture of the School and the Problem of Change'*, New York: Teachers College Press.

SHAKESHAFT, C. and PERRY, A. (1995) 'The language of power versus the language of empowerment: Gender differences in administrative communication', in CORSON, D. (Ed.) *Discourse and Power in Educational Organizations*, Cresskill, NJ: Hampton Press.

SHAPIRO, M. (1987) *The Politics of Representation*, Madison: University of Wisconsin Press.

SHILLING, C. (1992) 'Reconceptualizing structure and agency in the sociology of education', *British Journal of Sociology of Education*, **13**, 1, pp. 69–87.

SIKES, P.J. (1992) 'Imposed change and the experienced teacher', in FULLAN, M. and HARGREAVES, A. (Eds) *Teacher Development and Educational Change*, Falmer Press: London.

SIKES, P.J., MEASOR, L. and WOODS, P. (1985) *Teacher Careers: Crises and Continuities*, London: Falmer Press.

SIROTNIK, K. and OAKES, J. (1986) 'Critical inquiry for school renewal: Liberating theory and practice', in SIROTNIK, K. and OAKES, J. (Eds) *Critical Perspectives on the Organization and Improvement of Schooling*, Boston: Kluwer-Nijhoff.

SISKIN, L.S. (1994) *Realms of Knowledge: Academic Departments in Secondary Schools*, London: Falmer Press.

SMITH, M.S. and O'DAY, J. (1991) 'Systemic school reform', in FUHRMAN, S. and MALEN, B. (Eds) *The Politics of Curriculum and Testing*, London: Falmer Press.

STOLL, L. and FINK, D. (1996) *Changing our Schools*, London: Falmer Press.

References

STRAUSS, A. and CORBIN, J. (1990) *Basics of Qualitative Research: Grounded Theory Procedures and Techniques*, Newbury Park, CA: Sage.

STRINGFIELD, S., MILLSAP, M. and HERMAN, R. (1997) *Urban and Suburban/Rural Special Strategies for Educating Disadvantaged Children: Findings and Implications of a Longitudinal Study,* Washington, DC: US Department of Education.

TALBERT, J.E. and ENNIS, M. (1990) 'Teacher tracking: Exacerbating inequalities in the high school', Paper presented at the annual meeting of the American Educational Research Association, Boston, MA.

UCHIDA, A. (1992) 'When "difference" is "dominance": A critique of the "anti-power-based" cultural approach to sex differences', *Language in society*, **21**, pp. 547–68.

WEILER, K. (1988) *Women Teaching for Change: Gender, Class, and Power*, New York: Bergin and Garvey.

WELLS, A.S. (1991) 'The sociology of school choice: A study of black students' participation in a metropolitan voluntary transfer plan', unpublished doctoral dissertation, New York: Teachers College.

WELLS, A.S. and SERNA, I. (1996) 'The politics of culture: Understanding local political resistance to detracking in racially mixed schools', *Harvard Educational Review*, **66**, 1, pp. 93–118.

WELNER, K. and OAKES, J. (1996) '(Li)Ability grouping: The new susceptibility of school tracking systems to legal challenges', *Harvard Educational Review*, **66**, 3, 451–70.

WESTOBY, A. (1988) *Culture and Power in Educational Organizations*, Milton Keynes, England: Open University Press.

WIDEEN, M.F. (1994) *The Struggle for Change*, London: Falmer Press.

WILLIS, P. (1977) *Learning to Labor*, New York: Columbia University Press.

WODAK, R. (1995) 'Power, discourse, and styles of female leadership in school committee meetings', in CORSON, D. (Ed.) *Discourse and Power in Educational Organizations*, Cresskill, NJ: Hampton Press, pp. 31–54.

YIN, R. (1989) *Case Study Research*, Beverly Hills, CA: Sage Publications.

Index

ability grouping, 27
Acker, S., 3, 17, 21, 67
ACLU
  tracking, 28
administration
  Good Old Boys, 48
  leadership, 143–4
  styles, 18
  support, 128
adult-adult relationships, 21
Alexander, J., 11
Allen, B., 34, 38
  CLA program, 80
  Good Old Boys, 46–7, 77, 92–3
  Idea Team, 44–5, 68, 83, 86
  reform role, 38
  restructuring plan presentation, 85
altruism, 49
Anyon, J., 26
Apple, M.W., 14, 16, 17, 67
Arnold, J., 121, 122–3
Artiles, G., 65
assessment, 142–3
asymmetry of resources, 102–3
athletics *see* sports coaches

Bahktin, M., 4
balkanized cultures, 14, 69, 71, 73
Ball, S.J., 3, 14
  assertive women, 24, 79
  micropolitics, 19, 20–1
  political agendas, 15
  self-interest, 125
  teachers' definition of school, 3
Bathgate, B., 136
  Good Old Boys support, 101, 105
  history, 36
  Idea Team, 45

Baxter, T., 34, 36, 102
'Beachside' school
  heterogeneous grouping, 21
Beaufort, R., 36, 103–4
Berg, L., 49–50, 96
  detracking, 58
  heterogeneous grouping
    committee, 89
  Idea Team, 68
  restructuring plan, 84
  vision statement, 83
Berger, P., 23, 52
Berry, B., 21
Beyond Sorting and Stratification
  study, 27–33
Biklen, S.K., 24
Black, R., 110–11, 113, 114, 116
Blackmore, J., 2, 13, 15, 18, 24
Blase, J., 20, 21
board members, 101, 102
Boskey, R., 48, 60, 84, 96
  campus changes, 106
  Dream Team, 93
  gender bias, 55
  Idea Team commitment, 95
Braddock, J.H., 28
Brooks, G.H., 18
Brown, W., 53–4, 61, 65
Burton, D., 64, 91

calendar, 40–1, 70, 102–3
career opportunities, 17
caring, 64
Carnegie Foundation for the
  Advancement of Teaching,
  42
Carnegie Turning Points middle
  school model, 110

Carter, 114, 115
case studies
    Central High School, 1–108,
        124–9, 130, 131, 133, 135, 137
    Explorer Middle School, 109–18,
        124–9, 131
    Grant High School, 118–29, 135
    methodology, 29
Casey, K., 17, 18, 24
Central High School, 1–108, 130,
    131, 133
    comparison with Explorer and
        Grant, 124–9
    incrementalism, 137
    micropolitics, 135
Central Lifetime Achievers (CLA), 39,
    44, 52, 57, 80–2
CLA *see* Central Lifetime Achievers
Cohen, E., 54
collaboration, 63–4, 68
    Idea Team, 104
    teachers, 63–4, 104
commitment
    family, 17
    Idea Team, 95
    time, 72, 99
Common Destiny Alliance, 32
communication styles, 116–17
community, 142
community context Central High
    School, 35–7
conflict management, 101
constitutive theory of human action,
    23
conversations, 24
Cooper, B., 83, 98–9
    altruism, 49
    CLA program, 81
    heterogeneous grouping
        committee, 62–3
    integrated curriculum, 91–2
    reform aftermath, 106
Corbett, H.D., 12
Corbin, J., 32
Corson, D., 23

Crawford, M., 24, 25, 26
critical inquiry, 68
critical mass group, 44
critical pedagogy, 50
Cuban, L., 2
cultural political resistance, 50
culture, 11–12, 13–15, 37
    balkanized, 14, 69, 71, 73
    patriarchal, 37, 78–80, 85, 95,
        100
    subcultures, 14–15, 43, 68
Cummins, G., 63, 78–9
Cunnison, S., 79, 94, 98
curriculum, 142–3
    committee, 62–3
    differentiation, 27
curriculum change, 89
    English, 91
    math, 96–7
    science, 90
custom calendar, 40–1, 70, 102–3

Dalton, B., 101, 104, 106
    detracking, 60–1
    Idea Team, 84
    personal life, 50
    sports, 70
    union, 36
Danson, J., 114, 117
Darling-Hammond, L., 29
Darren, A., 64
Datnow, A., 4, 32, 139
Davis, J., 117
Davis, T., 105–6
Dawes, B., 116
Dawkins, M.P., 28
Dawson, J., 39–40, 94, 112–13
Deal, T.E., 11
decentralization, 10
decision making, 24
deconstruction, 11
demographics
    Central High School, 33–4
    Explorer Middle School, 109–10
    Grant High School, 118

Demsey, V., 21
departmental changes, 89–92
departmental overlaps, 127
desegregation, 28, 137
detracking, 1, 126
    Central High School, 27, 29–32, 40
    English, 90
    Explorer Middle School, 110–11
    Good Old Boys, 60–2, 67
    Grant High School, 118–24
    Idea Team, 58–9, 62–3
    interview questions, 146–7
    math, 91–2
    micropolitics, 133, 135
    Middle Group, 74–6
    science, 90
Dirty 13, 47
disadvantaged students, 53
discourse, 3
    Good Old Boys, 94–100
    Idea Team, 98–100
    organizations, 25
    power, 23, 24
    representation, 22
    sexist, 94–8, 107, 122, 124, 131
disempowerment, 79
district administrators, 47
district school board, 36
district superintendent, 101, 103–4
domesticity, 95–6
dominance, 24
Dream Team, 45, 93, 103, 136
Dreamers, 45, 125
Dreeben, R., 17

Earl, L., 2
elementary schooling, 16
Elmore, R., 1
emotional support, 64
empowered schools, 10
empowerment, 38, 50
English, 91, 118–19, 121, 123–4
Ennis, M., 31
Evans, K., 49, 90, 103

Explorer Middle School
    case study, 109–18, 131
    comparison with Central and Grant, 124–9

Facilitating Team, 45, 86–7
factionalism, 5, 21, 93
fairness, 70
family
    commitments, 17
    structure, 57–8
feminist pedagogy, 18
Fink, D., 11
Finley, M.K., 31, 42
Foster, B., 34, 37–8
    CLA group, 44
    conflict management, 101
    custom calendar, 102
    Dream Team, 93
    Middle Group, 86
    resignation, 104–5
    restructuring plan presentation, 84, 85
    sexual harassment, 100
    superintendent, 103–4
    teacher agency, 82–3
Foucault, M., 23
Fullan, M., 1, 10, 11, 13, 15, 59

Gamoran, A., 28, 31, 57
Gardner, H., 53
Gheradi, S., 24, 25
Giddens, A., 102
Gilligan, C., 64
Giroux, H.A., 14, 50, 68
Gitlin, A., 132
Good Old Boys, 1, 6, 37, 43–4, 125
    CLA program, 81–2
    committees, 87–8
    conclusion, 107–8
    detracking, 60–2, 67
    Foster's resignation, 104–5
    Idea Team's gender discourse, 98–100
    identity, 46–8

ideologies, 50–2, 66–7, 76–7
low student achievement, 57–8
micropolitics, 135–6
Middle Team view, 100–1
name, 46
outside support, 101
political strategies, 101–6
power, 78–80
power loss, 92–3
reform aftermath, 106–7
reform perspectives, 64–6
restructuring plans, 83–4, 85–6
sexist discourse, 94–8
student ability, 53–5
Goodson, I., 4
Gramsci, A., 18, 68, 92, 137
Grant High School
case study, 118–24
comparison with Central and
Explorer, 124–9
micropolitics, 133
Grant, R., 17
Gray, J., 24

Hanford, B., 119–20, 122, 123
Hargreaves, A., 89
collaborative cultures, 68
empowered schools, 10
innovative elite, 93, 135
politics, 2, 15
reculturing, 11
school culture, 12, 13
subcultures, 14
Heckman, P., 10
heterogeneous grouping, 40, 59
'Beachside' school, 21
committee, 62–3, 88–9
Explorer Middle School, 111,
112–13
Good Old Boys, 61
Grant High School, 120
Middle Group, 75
hierarchical power relationships, 11,
19
Hirshberg, D.B., 32, 129

Hochschild, J., 136–7
homeroom period, 40
homeroom teaching, 97
homogeneous grouping, 27
Hopkins, D., 10
house model, 40, 51, 63
Hoyle, E., 20
Huberman, M., 13, 32, 132

Iannaccone, L., 19, 20, 22
iceberg model, 116–17
Idea Team, 1, 6, 39–40
collaboration, 104
committees, 87–8
conclusion, 107–8
departmental change, 89–92
detracking, 58–9, 62–3
formation, 83
Foster's resignation, 104, 105
gender discourse, 98–100
Good Old Boys' sexist discourse,
94–8
identity, 43–5
ideologies, 48–50, 66–9, 76–7
low student achievement, 56–7
micropolitics, 135–6
name, 44–5
reform aftermath, 106–7
reform perspectives, 62–4
restructuring plan, 83–6
student ability, 52–3
superintendent approach, 103
idealism, 135–6
identities, 43–77
ideological themes, 23
ideologies, 3, 43–77, 132–3
classroom practice, 26
Explorer Middle School, 111–18
Grant High School, 119–24
Idea Team, 48–50, 66–9, 76–7
Middle Group, 72–6
overlap with gender, 125–6
school culture, 13–15
In House, 116, 125
incremental change strategy, 136–7

indigenous invention, 10
individualism, 142
information technology, 40
innovative elite, 93, 135
innuendo, 96
insider-outsider dilemma, 138, 139
institutional forces, 4
intelligence, 53–4, 121
    see also student ability
interactional norms, 24
interviews, 30–1, 140–7
isolation, 73

Jamison, T., 58–9
Jansen, B., 113–14
Jeffrey, M., 112
jigsaw method, 88
Johnson, C., 56
Johnson, M., 24
joking, 94, 101
Jones, B., 115

Kanpol, B., 50, 68
Kemper, D., 54
Kennedy, A., 11
Kenway, J., 2, 13, 15, 18, 24
Korn, F., 90
Kulik, C.C., 28
Kulik, J.A., 28

Labov, T., 23
Lakoff, G., 24
Lande, C., 77
language, 3, 23–4, 133–4
leadership, 18
learning disabled classification, 26
learning styles, 55
Lieberman, A., 11
life histories teachers, 62
Lipman, P., 11
Lipton, M., 30, 32
Lortie, D.C., 17
Luckmann, T., 23, 52

McLaren, P., 50, 68
McLaughlin, M.W., 14, 26, 67, 92
McNeil, L.M., 10
Malen, B., 20
Mangham, I., 2
Mann, P., 24, 108
marginalization, 126–7
Margonis, F., 132
Marsh, F., 38, 81
Marshall, C., 19, 23
math, 91–2, 96–7
Mead, G.H., 23
Mehan, H., 3, 4, 22, 23, 26, 108
Metz, M.H., 26
micropolitics, 2, 19–22, 23, 133–4, 137–8
The Micropolitics of the School: Towards a Theory of School Organization, 20–1
Middle Group, 6, 43, 44, 71–6, 77, 100–1
    committees, 87
    ideologies, 72–6
    incrementalism, 137
    restructuring plan presentation, 86
Miles, M., 13, 32
modes of representation, 22
Morris, H., 86
multicultural education, 143

Nathanson, C., 22, 23
Naysayers, 46
Nias, J., 13, 15, 21, 69
Noblit, G., 21

Oakes, J., 10, 27–30, 32, 41–2, 52, 57, 66, 68
O'Day, J., 10
Ogawa, R.T., 20
Okay Group, 71
O'Neil, J., 32
organization
    interview questions, 141–2
organizational theory, 19

organizations, 24
  discourse, 25
Owen, P., 55, 61, 84, 97

Page, R., 28, 31, 57
Parent Teacher Association, 35
parents
  contact, 145
  custom calendar, 102–3
  Good Old Boys support, 101
  Grant High School, 123–4
  politics of representation, 26
  use by factions, 127–8
passive resistance, 71
patriarchal culture, 37, 78–80, 85,
  95, 100
patriarchal structure, 112
pedagogy, 18, 142–3
peer-coaching, 40
Perez, J., 50
Perry, A., 17, 18, 64
Peterman, F., 10
politics of representation, 22–5, 26
power
  Good Old Boys, 78–80
  language connection, 23–4, 133–4
  as motivating source, 124–5
  politics, 98
  relationships, 11, 12, 19, 26,
    134–5
  students, 146
Power House, 113, 115–16
pragmatism, 135–6
promotion, 17

race, 144–5
  detracking, 75–6
  Good Old Boys, 54–5
  reform impact, 138
  student achievement, 110
  tracking correlation, 28
radical change strategy, 136–7
Ray, K.A., 32, 121, 129, 139
realpolitik, 136
reculturing, 12

reform perspectives, 62–6
Regan, H.B., 18, 64
representation, 3, 9
  modes, 22
  politics of, 22–5, 26
reputation
  Central High School, 34
Restine, N., 18, 64
Rich, A., 78
Ridell, S., 17
Rites of Passage (ROPES) curricular
  model, 116
Ropes House, 113, 115, 116, 117
Rossman, G., 12
Russo, B., 93, 102–3, 105
Ryan, J., 2

Sarason, S., 10, 13
  politics, 2
  power relationships, 12, 19, 26
  school culture, 11
  school location, 1
school board, 36, 47
school culture, 11–12, 13–15, 37
school efficacy, 142
school location, 1
school structure, 12
science, 90
Scribner, J., 19, 23
self-interest, 2
  Good Old Boys, 61–2
  Idea Team, 49, 95
Serna, I., 27
sexism, 16
sexist comments, 116
sexist discourse, 94–8, 107, 122,
  124, 131
sexist joking, 94, 101
sexist remarks, 125
sexual harassment, 97, 99–100, 101,
  125
Shakeshaft, C., 17, 18, 64
Shapiro, M., 22
Shilling, C., 44
Shiro, N., 51, 62, 90, 94–5, 96, 105

Sikes, P.J., 10, 15, 17, 62, 95
Simmons, P., 117
Sirotnik, K., 10, 68
Siskin, L.S., 2, 15, 67, 92
Sizer, T., 81
Skelly, J., 22, 23
skilled change agentry, 10
Smith, M.S., 10
social change, 18
social class, 28, 138
social construction, 52
social constructs, 24
social differentiation, 138
social location, 3, 4, 19, 22, 24
social status
    teachers, 42
social transformation, 50
special programs, 51
sports coaches, 37, 47, 69, 70
staffing, 141–2
stereotypes, 17, 94, 98, 117
Stoll, L., 11
Strauss, A., 32
Stringfield, S., 1
structure, 12
students
    ability, 52–5, 112, 121, 144–5
    achievement, 35, 56–8, 110
    disadvantaged, 53
    power, 146
subcultures, 14–15, 43, 68
superintendent, 101, 103–4
support, 40, 64
Swanson, D., 54

Talbert, J.E., 26, 31
teacher-centred approach, 11
teachers
    agency, 9–11, 37–8, 81, 82–3,
        132–3
    change initiation, 38
    collaboration, 63–4, 104
    consensus, 134
    detracking effects, 32

factionalism, 5, 21, 93
    identities, 43–77
    ideologies, 43–77
    interviews, 31
    life histories, 62
    personal experience, 59
    power relations, 19, 134–5
    role, 48–52, 73–4, 122
    social status, 42
    subcultures, 14–15
    time investment, 49
    tracking, 42
    training, 40, 110
    working conditions, 143
teachers' union, 35–6, 69, 70, 101
team teaching, 32, 51, 63, 111
Testosterone Trio, 122, 125
time commitment, 72, 99
time investment, 49
tracking, 27–9
traditional teaching, 60, 111, 115,
    117, 119–21, 128

Uchida, A., 24, 26
union, 35–6, 69, 70, 101

Walker, D., 63
Walker, T., 113, 117
Waters, D., 88
Weiler, K., 16, 18, 108, 138
Wells, A.S., 27, 29, 30, 66
Welner, K., 27
Westoby, A., 14
Wideen, M.F., 10, 13
Willis, P., 64
Winters, M., 96, 99
Wodak, R., 23
Wolf House, 113–15, 127–8
women's work, 16, 94, 96–7, 131
Wong, M., 47–8, 60
Wright, S., 118–19, 120, 122, 123

Yin, R., 29, 30, 32